Mastering
the **Craft** Ten Years
Of Weekes
1948–1958

"I had emerged from the Bridgetown poor, and by force of hard work, a focused mind, a scientific approach to my craft, I reached a position which the experts said was the top of the world. What did it mean? Well, for sure I was not in a position to do much about it. I certainly did not know how to convert my enormous status into property, and the WICBC, my employer, was not interested in fostering such a transition. The Board was in the hands of the rich and powerful in the region and saw players such as myself in a way that estate owners saw field hands. We were called to work, received a stipend on which we could not live, given a uniform that made us look the part, and when the job was done we were sent packing until required for the next year's crop."

Mastering
the # Craft Ten Years Of Weekes 1948–1958

Sir Everton DeCourcey Weekes
with Hilary McD Beckles

Universities of the Caribbean Press Inc

in association with the
C.L.R. James Centre for Cricket Research
University of the West Indies, Cave Hill Campus, Barbados

First publisherd in Jamaica, 2007 by
Universities of the Caribbean Press Inc.

© 2007 Everton DeCourcey Weekes

ISBN 978-976-952-011-0 (hbk)
        978-976-952-012-7 (pbk)

**A catalogue record for this book is available from the
National Library of Jamaica.**

Cover and book design by Shelly-Gail Folkes
Printed and bound in the United States of America.

Set in Bembo 12pt

In memory of Frank and Clyde

TABLE OF CONTENTS

Foreword / ix

Preface / xi

Acknowledgements / xii

Chapter 1
Born in a Village Academy / **1**

Chapter 2
Raised in the Shadow of Kensington / **22**

Chapter 3
The Mind Game: Mastering Technique and Method / **35**

Chapter 4
Beating BCA Ball: the Soldier Inside / **53**

Chapter 5
Storming Kensington: Representing Barbados / **69**

Chapter 6
Lost in Barbados: Found in Bombay / **87**

Chapter7
1950 in England: The End of Empire / **106**

Chapter 8
First Number One World Rating-1950 / **124**

Chapter 9
Second Number One World Rating -1956 / **132**

Chapter 10
Some Reflection on Today's Players / **170**

Commentaries:

- C.A. Jack Anderson / **187**
- Scyld Berry / **192**
- Charles Alleyne / **195**
- Sir Donald Bradman / **201**
- Peter West / **202**
- Richie Benaud / **206**

FOREWORD
BY THE RT. HON. OWEN ARTHUR

There are some things in one's life that stand out forever.

For me, one such occasion was my first attendance at a cricket Test Match – The West Indies versus Pakistan in 1958.

Across the vale of years, I can still vividly remember my first sight of Everton Weekes, and his magnificent 197 on that occasion.

To my childhood eyes, watching him bat was akin to witnessing a form of magic.

But there was something more and special to the occasion, it was the opportunity to see, in the flesh and at his best, a man who was, in every best regard, a legend and a hero to us, the young Barbadians of the 1950s.

We wanted to be like Weekes.

The Test career of Everton Weekes is an important, classical part of Barbados and West Indian social history. His excellence as a batsman and the great artistry and gallantry that he brought to the game were all an essential part of his contribution to cricket.

But there was about Weekes always something that was bigger and greater than his extraordinary skills as a player. He was of the Bridgetown poor, seeking a place for himself, and those of his class, in a society that was limited in the opportunities it offered, and socially rigid in the way in which those opportunities were created and extended. Through his excellence on the cricket field, Sir Everton helped in a fundamental way to change Barbados for the better, forever, by proving that true excellence cannot be constrained by social barriers.

And as early as 1950 he and the other members of the West Indies cricket team helped to start the process that led to the

'End of the Empire', as Constantine so eloquently termed it, by establishing that the people of these, our West Indian islands could better the British who, at the time, exercised political control over our affairs.

Everton Weekes' cricketing career was therefore an assertion of excellence from the grassroots at a time when that assertion was required as part of our general claim to rights of self determination.

Of course, there is much more to Sir Everton than his cricketing exploits. His remarkable intellect, his wonderful sense of humour, his sophistication in every respect have caused us to ponder as to the heights he could have scaled had the opportunities available to us today been available to him in his youth.

He has also, without fanfare and with little or no personal gain, provided sterling service to the game of cricket off the field, to his nation, and by his mentorship, to young aspiring Barbadian cricketers too numerous to mention. His story needed to be told. That it is now being told fills an important void not only in the cricketing but also the social history of Barbados.

And like everything with which Sir Everton has been associated, I am sure that it is a story that is told with a high wit, his characteristic graciousness and generosity of spirit – and above all with that special but indefinable touch of Barbadianess which marks him out as one of our greatest citizens of all time.

Owen Arthur
Prime Minister

PREFACE

Sir Everton Weekes' Test career spanned the period 1948 to 1958, hence the sub-title of this book "Ten years of Weekes". In these ten years he played 48 Tests for the West Indies. He scored 4,455 runs at an average of 58.61. He scored 15 centuries, the first five of which were consecutive, and the highest of which was 207. With Frank Worrell [51 Tests, ave. 49.48] and Clyde Walcott [44 Tests, ave. 56.68] he occupied the heartland of the first great West Indies Test team. He was known as the most formidable run scoring machine of his generation, and was twice rated (1950 and 1956) the best batsman in the world. His story is the quintessential tale of the Barbadian/West Indian journey from inner-city poverty to global excellence, and is told in a fashion that promotes the human desire for greatness of mind and generosity of spirit. This has been a labour of love. It is a manifesto statement of modern Caribbean Civilization. Every West Indian cricketer should read, absorb, and walk with its messages. At the centre of all things great resides a fine mind. Sir Everton possessed such an intellect which he used relentlessly in the service of West Indian cricket and society. There is no finer story of our times. Being a part of its telling has been the most rewarding literary experience of my life.

Hilary McD. Beckles

ACKNOWLEDGEMENTS

"Many people have urged for some time now that I consign the story of my Test career to book form. I have spoken about it on many occasions, and many things have been said by others. Early in 2006 I took the decision to proceed and approached Professor Hilary Beckles to facilitate. I sincerely wish to thank him for undertaking the project and bringing it to completion. Hours of taped recordings at the C.L.R James Centre for Cricket Research, Cave Hill Campus, UWI, enabled reflection and soul searching. Mrs. Grace Franklin worked on the typescript after transcribing a dozen tapes. Janet Caroo, research assistant, dug out forgotten material, and assisted the project team at the C.L.R James Centre. I wish to thank them all."

ONE

BORN IN
A VILLAGE ACADEMY

"LITTLE EVEE DIDN'T TURN OUT TOO BADLY", my mother Lenora used to say. She came to see me in a Test match at Kensington once, but I believe she was not surprised her 'little' son had dedicated his time and mind to mastering the craft of batsmanship. I don't think for a moment she thought my small size a problem for me in achieving anything I set out to do. She was proud of me and would tell people in the village that her "little Evee didn't do too badly".

I was mumma's only son, born on 26 February, 1925 in Pickwick Gap, in a typical chattel house in the inner city of Bridgetown. Maybe I was born to be a cricketer as I grew up on a street a ball's throw from the historical Kensington Oval which loomed large in my mind as a child. It was the only place within the community that captured my imagination. There was no museum, no library; just Kensington Oval, a place of legend. I was determined to find my way out in that middle, one way or another. All of the boys in the community had the same ambition.

Two years after I was born, 1927, the West Indies gained Test status and prepared for the inaugural tour to England. We played three matches against England in the summer of 1928 and were defeated 3-0. Maybe the coincidence of the dates, and result of the series, were signs that I was destined to be a Test cricketer who would fight for the respect of West Indies cricket. When England returned the tour in 1930 they played at Kensington Oval, and I am sure every one in Pickwick Gap, if they could have afforded it, would have found a way into the Oval. While I was learning the game on Pickwick Gap, my mother moved to a nearby area of the city called New Orleans. It was in this community, that contributed to the vibrancy of the inner city, that I was exposed daily to the art and science of cricket.

The folks in New Orleans had produced what was a cricket village academy. The narrow gaps, not wide enough to be called streets, were the natural spaces where as kids we played from sun-up until sun-down. There were professors of the game in the gap who knew all there was to know, and they graded the kids. By the age of ten I had played more hours of cricket than some Test players today on debut. It was not that we had nothing else to do. I have heard some players expressed the view that cricket was the only sport available in Barbados, hence their attachment to the game. Well, we had many distractions. The beach was an attractive place for all kinds of activities, including swimming, if you see what I mean. We played soccer, and other ball sports. But cricket was the game of the people. We preferred it because of its rich legacy, the attention paid to it by almost everyone in the community, and the strong adherence they paid to its rules and regulations.

Maybe that was where I came in, and got hooked. I loved anything that had a complex set of rules and regulations. I was attracted to activities that called for order, focus, and discipline. In the gaps between the fragile wooden houses, the kind of cricket we played called for all of these qualities. If, for example, you were batting and struck the ball in the air, hitting a house, you were given out. You then had to bowl your way back to the crease, if you wanted to bat again.

We had to learn to see within the mind the precise location of the gaps between the houses. It was a skill, and if you wanted to occupy the crease, you had to master it at an early age. The emphasis was on discipline, technique and method. This was the world I loved, and from an early age I became obsessed with mastering technique and method. The older chaps in the village would marvel at my commitment. Little boys were easily drawn into having a swing across the line and not to use a straight bat. There was something beautiful about learning to master the method of using a straight bat and keeping the ball along the ground.

I had one sister, and along with my mother and aunt, they heard quite a bit about my stamina at the crease. In those days, the word would spread like wild fire if a chap, at an early age, showed a tendency to play straight by getting behind the ball, especially against fast bowling. I was not afraid to get behind the ball because I discovered very early that it was the safer thing to do. If you were small, and had a highly developed sense of survival, as I did, then you got behind the ball and kept your eyes glued to it.

My aunt also invested her time in mothering my sister and I; she too was a strict disciplinarian. All of this came together, I suppose, in the making of my cricket mentality. When I became a Test cricketer and developed consistency, I would often try to understand what early influences went into the making of my mental approach. Each time I asked the question, I came down on the same side; an upbringing built around discipline, order, and respect for rules. This is not to say that I was not a little bit of a rebel. I got my share of the lashes that were handed out to unruly boys by parents in New Orleans. But I always knew why I got them, and in all fairness, I usually felt that each time I had done something to deserve them.

My family was poor but we placed a lot of emphasis on dignity. This might seem a bit of a cliché, but in those days poverty was devastating and crippling for grown folks. It would break the minds of many parents, while children seemed indifferent in the midst of games and other forms of recreation. I had no problems with the way I was being raised. I had a happy childhood. My father had emigrated to work in the oilfields of Trinidad, and would send some cash to keep the household afloat. My mother had a little kitchen garden that supplemented the budget.

My aunt was very supportive, and collectively we managed to keep the respect that some families could not maintain. I was 19 years before I was able to spend a little time with my father, and then I realized that I had inherited many of his characteristics. He was dedicated to traditional values; didn't play cricket in any serious way, but believed in giving the fullest application to the task at hand. I was surprised by how similar we were in approach; the power of genes, I supposed, because he was not there to shape my childhood experiences.

A Test cricket mentality is made up of a special blend of attitudes and aptitudes. More often than not these are forged in childhood, and sometimes they are discernible. You need to believe in your ability – physical, intellectual, and spiritual. The odds of your survival at the crease are not in your favor and so you need some kind of belief system, faith if you will, because some strange things can happen and you need to come up with an acceptable explanation. My childhood was rooted in Christian values, and I was socialized as a boy scout to practice them in everyday life.

I felt at an early age that comprehending all facets of life was beyond anyone's abilities. I therefore embraced God in order to make sense of the little part of it I had to deal with. Later I realized as a Test player that you sometimes needed a little help from above. One day you would feel that things were working out pretty good, and you would give a nod of acknowledgment. Sometimes the pickings were slim and you would ask a question.

I do believe it is important to place yourself in the wider scheme of things and understand you are but a small part of a divine order. Clarity of mind allows you to make decisions that show restraint, discipline, and respect. I learnt these things at home, in the cubs, in school, and in the church. I took them with me, like gear, on to the cricket field, and I believe they served me well. It was no easy matter being out there in the middle for ten years, performing at the top of the international game. My mental make-up was as vital to success as any technical skill I honed in the nets.

I attended St. Leonards Boys School, where boys from similar background as myself received a primary education in the basics of reading, writing and arithmetic. From the age of five until fourteen, I did my best to absorb the daily diet of a standard elementary curriculum that was more about England than the West Indies. It was a church-based school, with a heavy grounding in scriptures, as it was called then. When I walked out those gates for the last time, I was not sure what career I was prepared for. I did not work until I joined the army at the age of 17.

I refused the menial work my primary education prepared me for. The three years after leaving school were spent playing cricket, hanging around with friends on the beach, but nothing constructive in terms of crafting a livelihood. I became the first student from St. Leonards to play for Barbados, a status I held until very recently. I felt very proud when I received a letter from Headmaster Joe Clarke offering congratulations on my selection to the national side. It was a proud moment even though I had been out there in the community, without a skill, a job, or any form of employment.

My schooling did not empower me to escape the common poverty trap. It was the norm for 90% of working class boys to attend elementary school until the age of 14, and to leave for the fields, an artisan trade, or to provide general labour in the construction industry. I was no different from the majority of city boys who were generally assigned to a life of unemployment or seasonal employment. There was no prospect of going to secondary school without a scholarship or some other form of financial support.

But there were always other boys who appeared to have it more difficult than me, most of them having to walk barefooted and did not know where the next meal was coming from. I was aware of this entrapment, and was keen to find a way out. For many years as a professional cricketer I could still feel the effects of those three years. The absence of educational opportunity was something not easily ignored, but my determination to use the power of positive thinking in order to ensure that I would not be destroyed by the grip of poverty grew stronger with time.

City life was harsh on persons who were poor and vulnerable. Many who were sucked down by poverty knew that colonial society was unrelenting in ensuring there was a large pool of cheap labour for employers. There were communities such as Belleville and Strathclyde that were a part of elite society, and blacks who entered did so to labour, if their intentions were noble. I never looked upon these families and experienced any feeling of jealousy. They were over there, and I was over here. I knew why it was that way and I was supportive of those who wanted Barbados to have a fair and equitable society.

While I was keen to see an end to racial apartheid and class snobbery, when I interacted with the privileged classes I did not take their social advantages personally. I learnt as a youth to read the wicket, and to play each ball received on merit. That was my philosophy. First, I tried to understand the condition in which I found myself, and then develop methods to deal with it. I have met men in the cricket world from the elite in their societies who were decent to the core, lacking arrogance and prejudice, and I have known men from humble backgrounds who were keen to keep down another chap for no real reason other than a false sense of superiority.

My Test career rested upon these strong foundations. I believe my credentials as an apprentice were excellent, and that I was well prepared for the big game. It was a childhood preparation that entailed endless playing of the game, and community training in how to master the mental aspects. I made my debut at 13 years in the Barbados Cricket League (BCL) for a community team called Westshire. We lived in the west of the city, and Barbados was understood to be a 'shire' like Hampshire or Yorkshire. The BCL was in effect the organized nursery of working class talent that was to support Barbados and West Indies cricket.

Recently formed by the legendary Mitchie Hewitt, the BCL gave an opportunity to the poor boys to play competitive cricket within an organized environment. The Barbados Cricket Association, BCA, established at the end of the previous century, had acquired a reputation for catering to the white elite, the black and brown middle class, and a few from the financially secure clerical and artisan group within the working class. But the poor who could not afford to purchase gear were picked up by the BCL and nurtured to international standards. I was there along with many players who established international reputations such as Gary Sobers, Charlie Griffith, Seymour Nurse, Conrad Hunte and many others.

I was just five foot, barely tall enough to peep over the pads, when I started to play in the BCL. I was the youngest person to play in this competition. My cousin was a seasoned player for Westshire, a wanderers' side because it had no home ground. He looked after me as we toured and played teams in other parishes. Matches were played mostly on Thursday afternoon, so there was no interruption of my schooling. My cousin was an effective mentor the way he took care of my entry into the competitive game, and his belief that I would one day master the craft of batting. I believe he saw a way to build my character through weekly exposure to older players in different parts of the island. I knew he thought I had a future in the big game, but he never said. I can say though that he expected me to pull my weight in the team, even though I was just a pint-sized kid.

There were three aspects to my BCL years that provided me with the tools to survive with dignity and productivity at the international level. The first was discovering the keys to learning how to read a game, all of its internal aspects, including the pitch, atmosphere, and bowlers' ability. This was the first rule of cricket; read accurately the state of affairs and act on the knowledge gathered. In those days pitches were not covered, and were often under-prepared. You could not arrive at a ground with any set expectations.

The first thing you did on arrival was to have a good look at the pitch. Very rarely was the playing surface flat; most were sloped, sometimes with just about six yards in front of the crease prepared; the middle of the pitch could easily look like an open field on which sheep could graze. Sometimes the fast bowlers had no run-up to speak of. They would find a way to the wicket, and were often lethal. Most grounds were so small everyone fitted into a 20 yards radius. It was a rough, and very tough beginning.

I batted low in the order. But this made no difference to the hostility I received from fast bowlers. The culture in those days was for fast bowlers to test a youngster with fire and brimstone. A chap bowling at 80 miles an hour on a rough surface would try to take my head off just to see whether I was going to run to square leg, or continue all the way to the nearest bus stop.

No concession granted on the grounds of age, week after week I faced some pretty hostile stuff. You would be walking in to bat and a fielder would say, " hey kid, take this handkerchief and wipe the breast milk from the corners of your mouth". Sometimes there was a call from the crowd to "send the boy to the barbers", meaning of course to clip my ears.

The BCL built up a reputation for this kind of stuff. It was like the Roman gladiator ring where they pitched in the disposable. If you survived, you had a chance of winning your freedom and becoming a respected citizen. Well, I liked the thought of being a free citizen so I read the conditions, and applied the techniques learnt in the village gaps. I soon developed a reputation as the 'little man' who got in line and pushed the ball around. I was certainly not strong enough to hit it out the park, in any case it was not wise to do so. The 20 and 30 runs I would score were good enough to win respect from adults, and that was fine for me. By the time I had reached sixteen it was dawning on me that I had the ability to step to the next level, into the BCA, and to play for Barbados.

I would hear the older boys saying that the "little Weekes boy", with a few more dumplings, could make a good batsman. The assessment gradually seeped into my mind, and I began to believe what was being rumored. It was a slow creeping kind of self realization. A few 30s in the BCL and the word was out that I had passed the village test. In those days the professors in the gap were harsh on the shortcomings of every kid.

The second skill I acquired was knowing how to concentrate harder and longer the bigger the crowd, and the more important the game. In the BCL matches entire villages would come out to support their team, and some crowds were very vocal; what they would shout was not always complimentary to you or your mother. The language was often tinged with threatening references, not the kind of stuff you heard in Sunday school. You had to deflect it all, and focus on the business at hand.

Being a little on the small side encouraged fast bowlers when I was at the crease; some of them could imagine my blood being spilt on the pitch. So my innings were often like lion taming exercises; my task was to extract teeth or reduce the growl. Sometimes a fast bowler, broken in spirit by my defense, would admit that I was "a tough little......". That was the compliment I looked forward to receiving, earning it the hard way in front of large, rowdy opposition crowds.

Third, there was the importance of reducing risks in order to survive, while being sufficiently aggressive to dominate. This was not an easy matter. Some hard decisions had to be made. I liked batting. I did not like getting out. I did not like sitting on the bench watching a game in which I had failed to make a contribution. So I was determined to occupy the crease by reading conditions, eliminating ways of getting out, and climbing on top of bowlers in order to wear them down. It required patience with your skill, and knowing when to cut loose without losing balance and poise. I was therefore not an air force man, but a ground soldier.

By the age of 16 my personal law of batting was clear; if you hit the ball on the ground they would not be able to catch you. Eleven men are trying to catch a ball from my bat. These are simply yet profound truths. I therefore decided that I would not score runs by hitting the ball in the air. I would get my pleasure from watching eleven enemies chase it along the turf. Once I had decided to minimize the chances of getting out, it meant I had to enhance other run scoring strategies. Placement and timing became as important as power. I soon learnt how to use the pace of a fast bowler to beat the field, and how to 'dance' down to spinners and drive the ball straight in order to neutralize all fielders backward of square.

The Test arena was the place where I applied these principles and techniques with the most productive benefits. Westshire gave me the opportunity to learn the higher aspects of the game, and to appreciate its values as a way of life. I had no doubt that the cricket rules and regulations I learnt to respect were applicable to life in general. For sure, cricket taught some hard lessons about nature and people, and I discovered that as a game it is as sweet and painful as life itself.

The earlier these things are understood and applied by a young player, the better. I was fortunate to have entered a world of men as a youth and to acquire 'big people' knowledge before I was ready to shave. In effect, it happened because I was ready to learn by listening and assessing. I did not swallow all I heard. I learned how to be critical in my thinking and to separate useful information from 'old talk and fables'.

It was during my mid-teens that I discovered the joys of reading. I read mostly anything on sports I could get my hands on. I was fascinated by sportsmen who were able to live humbly with celebrity status, and managed the pressure of performance. Soccer players, golfers, tennis players and racing drivers were larger than life in the West Indies, more so than the cricketers who were local heroes.

From sports I moved on to literature, and developed an appetite for novels and biographies. Reading was not only a form of relaxation, it was a stimulating way to escape the rough edges of life in the inner city where some unsavory things could happen daily, spoiling the beauty of community life to which we were committed. In time I came to realize that reading was an extension of my general interest in building a disciplined approach to life, and strengthening my mental capacity in order to concentrate harder and longer.

There were few sports heroes within our reach. West Indies cricket had produced many great players, and Barbados especially had a larger share than its population suggests. There was a long tradition of home grown batsmen, from the era of H.G.B. Austin and George Challenor who unfortunately were past their best when West Indies received Test status in 1927. Also, there was a battery of excellent fast bowlers, including Herman Griffith, Manny Martindale, and George Francis.

Learie Constantine from Trinidad was a legend during my youth, though his Test record was not very impressive. He was a great ambassador for the game, loved in England where he had shown the county circuit what exciting West Indian batting, bowling and fielding was all about. We heard of his exploits on radio and read about them in the newspapers, and felt proud as youngsters that a West Indian was rated by some pundits as the most spectacular cricketer on the planet.

But my teenage hero was the great George Headley, 'Mas George' the Jamaicans called him, the 'Atlas' who carried West Indies cricket on his shoulder with the bat. "Mas George" was a small man, dapper in appearance, and always very neatly turned out. He was economical with words, and on the field he seemed effortless in his efficient accumulation of runs. We were aware he was the first great batsman the West Indies had produced at the Test level, and this was big news in the villages because in those days the division of labor was for whites to bat and blacks to bowl. "Mas George" as the greatest batman in the side, if not the world, was revolutionary; he was so young and brilliant. He certainly captured my imagination, and more than any other player represented proof that a working class boy with no higher education could make it to the top in cricket, and through self education establish a reputation as a gentleman.

The first time I saw 'Mas George' was in a Test match, the first game of the English tour in the West Indies in the 1934/35 series. There was a lot of talk in the village about the series. George was in his prime and England's Wally Hammond was not far behind in terms of reputation. I wasn't yet ten years old but there was so much discussion in the Gap about the cricket I thought I knew as much about it as anyone else. Everywhere in the village cricket talk dominated conversation, and my ears were never far away from a cricket discussion. Some of the older heads would say that it was nothing but racism and elitism that G.C. Grant, a white Trinidadian who was a Cambridge University student, should captain the Great Man. Everyone in the Caribbean who had any sense of fairness knew that this was wrong, but in Barbados, the Caribbean heartland of racism, such things were the norm.

And what a match it was! The West Indies team was taken apart in three days. What hurt us was not that we had lost the game; it was the manner in which we lost. The West Indies were bundled out for 102 on a wet, uncovered pitch, in the first inning, with George hitting 44 before he was run out. The next highest score was L.G. Hylton's 15 runs batting at no. 8. The West Indies in turn bowled out England for a miserable 81, Hammond top scoring with 43. With a lead of

21, the West Indies, carrying injuries, declared on 51 for 6, giving England a mere 73 to win which were knocked off for the loss of 6 wickets, Hammond again top scoring with 29 not out batting at no. 3. That was my introduction to Test cricket, but I had seen my hero playing a classy innings, holding up an end while chaos was reigning at the other.

When in 1937 the workers' rebellion broke out in Bridgetown, and New Orleans found itself in the centre of things, I was too young to fully understand the details, but I knew instinctively that it had to do with the unfair treatment working class folks were experiencing. There was a lot of hunger and poverty in the city, and poor folks had a hard time finding meals for themselves and children. Clement Payne's was the workers' leader and he spoke about the disenfranchisement of the poor. But for the elite he was just a dangerous trouble maker and a disturber of the peace. In New Orleans the poor could sink no further. This much was known to Payne who I recalled was able to pull some very large crowds to his political meetings.

Cricket and politics were at the center of conversations in the Gap. Discussions took many forms but they were always about the need to create greater opportunities for the working people, and putting an end to race and class discrimination. George was as much a hero as Clement Payne. My childhood was sandwiched between these twin towers of black struggle for justice. As was my inclination, I tried to understand it all. I would ask questions and listen to what was being said. My mother did much the same. Her concern was to make sure that poverty did not rob us of our dignity and self respect. Keeping out of trouble was her way of putting things; meaning that I was not to run foul of the law. The community had high expectation of the future, and I was doing my best to be a part of it.

Family life had a great deal to do with how I went about building my life as well as cricket innings. I worked hard at understanding the nature of everything around me, and within. I tried to be as clear as possible, given my age and limited social exposure. On reflection it was my commitment to clarity of thought, at an early age, that had much to do with the nature of my batting. By understanding the patterns of social life I could make some sense of the issues within and beyond the boundary that were to shape my performance as a cricketer.

I knew how important it was to discover ways in which to express my opposition to the social state of affairs, and cricket was the arena within which I could say what I had to say. In this regard I was very much influenced by "Mas George" who adopted a similar approach. It meant showing that excellence existed within the village, among the poor. This was my project, and I went about it as clinically as I could.

The society of the 1930s and 1940s was not designed to give working class people like myself much support in pursuit of careers that conferred honour and status. In fact, it was to the contrary. It was a place where a chap from the poor households, whose family came from the plantation at one stage or another, was not expected to wonder too far away from the field, just in case he was required to return. You were not expected to acquire skills that took you too far away from the needs of the sugar field and factories because it would be said that you had broken free. You could acquire a few skills in some areas, but you were expected to remain on the edge of the labour market.

It was a West Indian arrangement. It had to do with how far we had reached in terms of getting away from the plantation past that was not very pleasant. Many of the BCL clubs I played against were situated on plantation tenantries, and players were mostly field workers. In rural St. Michael, and other parishes, BCL teams were built by cane cutters who were fit young men who loved the game. They respected cricket because it was built on the principle of equality and justice for all, and offered respect to achievers. This meant a great deal to young men who were daily degraded by the drudgery of the cane fields.

The poverty we experienced had to do more with this history than with our ability as a people. I grew up surrounded by some very gifted and bright people whose ability was well known and who in a different, more humane circumstance, would have been outstanding citizens in terms of their contribution to human advancement. I was blessed, endowed I suppose, like many of my fellow villagers, with a little gift; a mind that enabled me to concentrate for long periods, and to apply it in ways that supported my desire to be a disciplined person. In those days a chap was known to have a mind that was 'tidy' or 'untidy', and whatever it contained on the inside was said to give shape and form to what was on the outside. It seemed clear to me as a teenager that a focused mind would create a disciplined approach to life, and that if I wished to be a cricketer at any level I would have to show that mental discipline was my number one skill.

My mother would frequently say that all you needed to know about people was what was occupying their mind. She knew that when I was about to play cricket there was nothing else on my mind. Sometimes she would be talking to me and I would not hear a word she said. I got a lot of knocks around my head for that, but I was often busy working out batting techniques and methods. And the more I concentrated the deeper into a trance I went. I would make up my mind not to play a specific stroke or do a certain thing at the wicket, and then apply the necessary methods in order to build long innings.

Once I had made up my mind it was a little difficult to have it changed. That made me a stubborn little fellow, but it was the way I knew how to deal with the odds, and to be consistent. I knew at an early age that if you were not in control of your mind, you could not be in control of your stay at the crease. While for adults this would seem like common sense, for a 15 year old it was like rocket science and I pride myself in being a budding little cricket scientist.

It is true what is said about personality traits in an individual. In most cases it begins in the home with parenting. It has little to do with parents unleashing excess discipline upon the kids. In my village I saw many of my mates being exposed to physical and psychological abuse excused as discipline. True discipline had more to do with how the time, a kid has, is organized into task and routines that call for personal management and respect for time frames. My mother was determined to ensure that my time was never so open as to allow me to live without constraints. I had things to do, in and about the house, which meant that I was under constant domestic guidance. I would hear her twice an hour saying, "Evee, come here and do this, and go there"! That sort of regime meant that I was taking instruction; that I was a part of the family team; and that if I did not do what was expected, I was letting the side down which resulted in a fair share of shame and guilt. Sometimes I thought that my mother was inventing chores for me in order to make sure that my brain was always active in a positive way.

The thought that I would end up before a magistrate answering personal questions was unbearable for my mother. There were few legitimate opportunities available to young men and women in my circumstance and it would have been like shooting oneself in the foot to do things that reduced even further the chances of enhancing one's prospects. That I had thought these things out in the way I did suggests I was reading the wicket I had to bat on, and was determined to maximize my life chances.

I was cautious about the society that was determined to deal harshly with me. If my small size did not matter to me, I did not see why my race should to anyone. I did not see the problems of my life as existing within me. They were out there, everywhere, and since I was raised to have confidence on the inside, then I had only the external challenges to deal with.

It was important to me that I was clear on these matters because when I walked out to bat, to face the uncertainty of the situation before me, I needed to be clear on one thing; that no one out there was superior to me in terms of my self-esteem and self worth. It had nothing to do with conceit or arrogance. I was encountering men around the world who had greater wealth, more extensive education, and the confidence bred of elite upbringing, but in the space called a cricket field my state of mind neutralized all of those advantages and enabled me to perform as an equal.

A serious player has to know who he is on the inside. If you are weak, and feel insecure as a person, it shows on the outside, and the opposition, smelling a wounded soul, will rise up and eat you alive. Likewise, if you are confident it leads to respect from the opposition. It was as much a mind game then as it is now. In my time, especially against England and India, we were up against national elites, men of property, higher education, and titles, and who had the full backing of their societies and governments.

My roots in the inner city of Bridgetown were strong, buried deep within the survival history of the people who had just ten years before rebelled in order to get British colonialism off their backs. I was to be a beneficiary of all that, and in a deep spiritual way I felt that I was a village ambassador of the hopes and aspirations held by the common people. When I went out to bat I was carrying all of this in my mind. I did not carry it on my back because it was not a burden. It was an honour to emerge from the same community that had risen up in support of Clement Payne in search of freedom and opportunities. Even if I did not fully interpret this as a political matter, I felt it inside which was enough to make the point that I was reflecting the confidence of the men and women of my time about the future.

The details of this situation are interesting from today's perspective. Some of my contemporaries did not handle these challenges very well, and I knew it had a little to do with the roll of the dice. But we faced a lot of pressure from class oppression, and race was an important part of it. I was socialized to take people as I experienced them, and not to pre-judge. If a chap was white or wealthy I engaged him as he related to me and others around me, and did not make prior judgments. This is how I learnt to play my cricket. I did not prejudge a bowler or pitch. I would wait to see how they behave, and I would adjust to suit.

I supposed it has to do with the Christian idea of 'judge not lest ye be judged'. This way I made many good friendships in my Test playing years from different races and class background. Some of these friendships are still strong today. It is also true that I met some pretty difficult chaps, and they too have remained that way. But the key, I would tell those who asked me, is to use your critical judgment and read people and circumstances to the best of your ability.

This principle found its way into my approach to the game. I was an impulsive reader of playing conditions and circumstances. This was my way. Youngsters today like to distract themselves with music, before, during and after a game. If this works for them, so be it. But for me, I needed to feel that my mind was creatively engaged, stimulated by reading, assessing and reflecting. I am as much a bridge player as a cricketer. Maybe this is the difference.

TWO

RAISED IN
THE SHADOW OF
KENSINGTON

I WAS BORN IN PICKWICK GAP, a stone's throw from Kensington Oval, the home of the Pickwick Club. If I had a first choice to play for a club in the competition organized by the BCA, it would have been Pickwick. But that was not to be. It was socially impossible during the 1940s. The Pickwick Club was a white only members club, as was the case in South Africa during apartheid. Colonial Barbados had practiced its own version of race apartheid after slavery was abolished in 1838. The legacies of slavery remained strong during my youth. They were challenged by the organized labour movement and radical politicians and intellectuals, not to mention ordinary men and women who considered the injustices they suffered unchristian. But racism persisted, and was still very potent. The Pickwick club, established in 1881, was over fifty years old, and had no black members. I was born and bred in its shadow, and like the Great China Wall, it seemed formidable.

I was born then in the thick of things; at the heart of West Indies cricket. In cricket terms that should have meant that I was born with a golden spoon in my mouth. As it turned out that spoon was made of some other less impressive material. I saw the great players of my time walking in and out of the Caribbean Mecca. I imagined that I would be one of them, and had all the usual fantasies of boys of my generation.

But there was this wall, this barrier which meant that if I entered the club I would be doing so as a pitch labourer, doing fielding chores, but not as a player. But it did not break my spirit. It did not dampen my enthusiasm for the game. I knew that it was wrong, and that there were people in the society who were struggling to do something about it, but the walls were not breached during my youth. I had to find another way. There is a saying that water always finds a way because it must flow. Well, that is how it was in my youth.

As I progressed into my teens, I knew that sooner or later I would make the transition into the BCA. Though I did not occupy myself too much with joining a club, I knew there were opportunities, as well as restrictions, based on my social condition rather than my ability. I was determined not to allow these prejudices to scar my character.

It was within this circumstance, at the age of 17 years, that I joined the Army. In a sense it seemed a logical thing to do. I could not join the civil service because I was not armed with high school certification. Unlike some of my contemporaries I did not have the benefit of that solid Barbadian secondary education that took many cricketers a great distance in life. Neither was I blessed with family connection and friendship ties that could open doors to a secure livelihood.

The army was a good place to begin the process of building

the foundation I needed to become a serious cricketer and to strengthen the mentality needed to prepare for adult life. I soon realized that there were opportunities to improve my general knowledge and living condition. There were avenues for educational advancement, and I was keen to gain on the corner what was not available on the straight. I took a deep dive into the classics of English literature, and found a source of great pleasure and relaxation. There were times when I wondered what my destiny would have been were I exposed to higher education, but each time I concluded that there were strong advantages in being self-taught.

My army years were vital in shaping the type of professional cricketer I became. The British army was a global institution, dedicated to winning imperial wars, not only against the Nazis and Fascists in Europe, but against the nationalists in Africa and Asia who were fighting to win their independence. All over the world, people wanted to throw British colonizers out of their countries. We heard a great deal about how Mahatma Gandhi marched a million barefooted Indians down to Government House and told the British Governor that the time had come for him to go home. While I did not leave Barbados and was not a part of any combat, I knew from the general information that circulated, that there was a very big world out there to which I was a part, and that if I wanted my piece of the action I had to stand up for it.

The army, then, provided me with considerable exposure in international affairs. When I became a Test cricketer I had acquired a reasonable working knowledge of the world that enabled me to analyze conditions in different countries. I sometimes wonder how young men today from the working class prepare themselves for these situations without formal education. In my coaching days after my Test career I would place emphasis on encouraging boys to build their awareness of the world, and most importantly, of themselves. Test cricket is a vigorous mental process and if you fail the exam within the community you are unlikely to pass it at the wicket.

I quite fancied the idea of staying in the army and having a crack at a military career. I enjoyed the discipline of army life at the time. Maybe the absence of combat had something to do with it. But the nature of the training I received suited my disposition. As a stickler for discipline and planning, the routines and ritual of the military blended with what I knew about myself. I found it very interesting having to get up early in the mornings, put in a few hours of physical training, and go to classes just after breakfast.

Equally important was the protection I received from abject poverty. For the first time I did not have to worry about where a meal was coming from. I exercised, played cricket and football, all the sports that interested me, and got time off to spend with my family. It really suited me to join the Army at that time. It was a way out of confinement. I could not risk waiting to become a civil servant. In any event, there was a small matter of having to pass exams.

I was invited by Harold Griffith to join Empire Cricket Club before I came out of the Army in 1947. At a later date I got a letter from the Secretary of the Pickwick Club asking, telling me in fact, that it was unanimously agreed that I be invited to become an honorary life member of the Club. Over a couple of drinks at Kensington I asked him if he would like to rewrite this letter because I thought it could only be unanimous if they had asked me if I would like to be a member of the Club. Of course some people thought I was rude. Then

I got another letter asking me if I would wish to be an honorary life member of the Club. I accepted and the matter was settled. By then many things had turned around in a way that I could not have imagined as a youth.

There is no doubt that for many years we had some very talented people in the Barbados Cricket League, many before me, who never got an opportunity or chance to play for Barbados. I used to watch the annual game of the BCL against the BCA and I could see that many in the BCA team were less talented than in the BCL, but class and race snobbery against the BCL by BCA officials blocked the roads into the Barbados team. BCL players, then, saw Kensington as a Bastille to be stormed if they wanted to have the honour of representing their country.

In my mid-teens I was often asked to work as a substitute fielder for the Pickwick team. In effect it was unpaid child labour, but I was keen to feel the air of the BCA game. When, for example, they were playing against Spartan or Empire, and somebody did not turn up on time, they would ask me to field. My reputation in the BCL had pushed me into the view of the BCA fraternity. I was not in high school and therefore had time to spare during the day. Were I in high school at that time I would have been playing with or against the likes of Frank Worrell and Clyde Walcott who, as teenagers, played in the BCA for Combermere and Harrison College respectively.

I made my debut in the BCA after joining the army. From the Garrison Sports Club X1, I made it into the Barbados team at age 19. As a Pickwick 'field hand', I had spent some time in Kensington where persons in positions of authority in the Barbados selection process knew something of my ability and aptitude. I would not say that I was discovered, in a dramatic sort of way, but it has been said that one or two Pickwick players might have had something to do with my being called to trials.

I went to trials in 1944 and got a lot of runs, more than anybody else, in fact. In the third game, after making 60 on one side I was asked to bat the same afternoon for the other side. I opened the innings, and I got 80-odd. But the impression I had at the time was that there was one available place in the team, and I was competing for it with somebody else who was preferred. It occurred to me that I was being given opportunities to fail. I was offered the place. Several years later I was told that the other person was favoured. He was not a bad player and quite a decent gentleman as well. He has now passed on. But he did say to me that it would have been unfair for him to have been selected over me because it would not have been on merit.

God smiled. I was not discarded, I was offered a chance, against the odds, to have a crack at the big game. I was determined to make the best of the chance presented me. I saw it almost as a sacred duty to perform on behalf of all those I knew who were very good but for whom no doors were opened. Sometimes life presents these burdens which you must carry, and once you know why, you carry them with honour and dignity. That is how I saw my entry into the Barbados team.

I knew that the path to national representation would not be smooth. I headed into the Barbados team without the experience of being a schoolboy player in the BCA which was the normal route for most young players. I was coming up through the flooring or through the back door. The army was not a conventional place to begin, and my friends wasted no time in telling me that I owed it to them to out perform the main track boys whose journey to the national side seemed well planned and prepared.

Not being a schoolboy player, in the sense that I never represented a distinguished school, posed no special problem for me other than being denied the prestige, I suppose, of having my name etched on a school wall alongside many of the greats of Barbados and West Indies cricket. Combermere, Lodge and Harrison's especially were nurseries of Barbados cricket. From these school teams players who did not make the Barbados or West Indies team went on to distinguished careers in government, the professions, and the private sector. I had been playing with adults from the age of 13 when I competed in the BCL. But this was a good thing in the sense that I was thrown into the deep end of adult competition and had an invaluable learning experience. It was not bookish learning but for sure it was first class exposure to the high science of the game.

I was exposed, however, to the negative side of the national cricket culture; not having the name of a distinguished school behind me, and therefore no alumni network to assist. I was vulnerable to the class and race divisions that haunted cricket selection. I was prepared to some extent to deal with this. After all, I was born in the shadow of the Pickwick club and Kensington Oval, but was not eligible to participate on racial grounds. So I lacked the credentials other than the fact that I was not bad with the bat. But I knew that in many instances such a skill was not enough to gain selection.

It started in the first trial games I played. I knew I had to make a lot of runs. And I did. Even then, it was still not clear that my selection was assured. I was told that the only way to seal the selection was to score more runs than anyone else in the very last game, and I did. I was up against the race barrier, and like working class black boys the world over at that time, I had to over perform in order to beat the elite to the crease. I knew this story well. We had heard about it as children in American sports, boxing and baseball especially. The Americans had established the Negro Leagues to deal with this matter in their own way, but they could not deny the power of merit to gain respect across all social boundaries.

During my four years with the Army I worked at building my reputation as a batsman, playing against established teams such as Spartan, Wanderers, Empire and the Police. At the same time I watched the West Indies team whenever it played at Kensington. 'Mas George', of course, remained my hero ten years after I saw him in 1934. He didn't have the classical, orthodox stance, but like many prolific batsmen he got into the orthodox position very quickly before playing the ball. If you watch his feet closely, you would notice the transition. His feet were very mobile as the bowler moved in, but he kept a steady head, which was critical.

As a batsman I tended to look to other batsmen as role models but I was very impressed with the quick man of Barbados and West Indies cricket, George Francis. I knew Francis in my youth because he lived in New Orleans, just a few gaps away from my home. He was a hero to all the boys in the area and we marveled at his pace. That he toured England with the West Indies made him a man of legend to us. Can you imagine living in a community with the fastest man on the island who had played cricket in England and Australia? During the 1930/31 tour to Australia the great Don Bradman was bowled by Herman Griffith in the fifth Test at Sydney for 0, but in the second Test, also at Sydney, Francis had taken him out, caught behind by keeper Ivan Barrow for 25. Also, in the first innings of the fifth Test when the Don scored 43, he was caught Francis bowled Martin.

As teenagers we knew these things. I had a role model just around the corner who had gone the distance. Boys from the Gap therefore had good reason to feel encouraged as young prospects. And of course there was also the famous Manny Martindale who shared the new ball with Francis for the West Indies during the 1930s. Manny was very quick, and I was happy to come along during the 1940s.

But the bowler I liked most of all was Bertie Clarke, the spinner. I had seen a lot of good off-spinners and leg-spinners in the BCL, but none of them got to trials for Barbados. All sort of excuses were made as to why these players were not called to trials. It was said, for example, that they could not bowl in boots, and that they could only perform in pumps and soft shoes. It was said that the batsmen were not disciplined, but it seemed to me that you could not make hundreds if you were not disciplined. The BCL pitches were not the best in the world for batting, and even if the bowlers were not the best, scoring a century called for a lot of concentration.

But there was a lot of discrimination in the Barbados selection process, and it existed for a while after my debut. When you are honest and talk about it some people still get angry, and preferred if it was wiped under the carpet. I've lived it and it didn't bother me because it was so common you got accustomed to dealing with it. You fought it the best way you could with your own influence but it had its supporters in high places and was difficult to uproot. When I became a Test player I had long taken a decision not to absorb any personal invective, and after a while people got to realize that I was a no-nonsense person who had no time to waste with anti-social attitudes and values.

While scoring heavily for the Garrison Sports Club the idea of playing for the West Indies began to creep into my consciousness. I started to look at some of the other players who were making runs and I kept saying to myself 'I believe I could make it like some of these people'. Frank and Clyde were in the same age group, but had made their names in the BCA. I would see in the Sunday papers that these boys, like me, were making 20 and 30 and the occasional 50. But I was playing on less well prepared pitches and figured that I could do much better on first class pitches.

I invested a great deal of energy in mastering technique and strengthening my mind game. I knew that if I wanted to be an effective player I needed to be confident in saying 'this bowler is not going to get me out'. After making this decision I would then work on the plan to get some runs. It meant trying new ideas and consolidating well tested methods. I knew that on good wickets I would be sufficiently versatile to score heavily.

Learning to adapt to a wide range of conditions is a critical skill. The BCL provided the experience of diversity. In the BCA considerable effort went into creating standard pitches that were fast and true. When I got into the Barbados and West Indies teams I had played on a wider variety of pitches than most of my colleagues. In the BCL I practiced the art of leg movements, and felt comfortable with dancing down the track. I developed a love of moving down to spinners and hitting them where I wanted. But of course I did not dance down the track unless I knew what was happening with the ball. So reading the spin of the ball was an important first step. If you couldn't read it was best to stay at home otherwise you would get lost, and worse yet, look lost.

It is often said that a problem with today's players is that they don't use their feet. But why would you use your feet if you don't know which way the ball is going? It makes no sense to me to leave the station if you do not know where the train is going. Learning to read the signs is therefore a vital component of batting. Some of the BCL surfaces on which I played as a teenager gave me the confidence to feel mobile at the crease. In learning to read I went about it very deliberately. I would find myself in the company of players who were doing well with the bat. I read magazines and newspaper interviews and tried to understand the strategies used by the great players.

The confidence of good friendships, and comfort with the gear are vital parts of the preparation of a young sportsman. As a teenager my good friend was Eric Crichlow who attended Combermere. We are still good friends today. He would leave school and play with me in the BCL. I thought he was good enough to play for Combermere. He and Frank were also close. When I made it into the BCA the army provided me with my first bag of proper playing equipment. I received a pair of white trousers, not flannel, and two proper white shirts. I wore a handkerchief around my neck to keep the shirt collar clean. Of course people used to think it was style, but it was more economics than fashion. I was not over-burdened with clothes at that point. Everything had to be handled carefully to ensure that it went the distance.

I got my first pair of canvas boots in 1947. Luckily for me when I was leaving the Army in that year they gave me a full cricket kit as a parting gift. While I was in I bought on credit a second-hand bicycle for 20 dollars. It took me nearly a year to pay for it. The loan was from Lieutenant Leonard Banfield. He said to me: 'Son, it doesn't matter how long it takes, but you have to repay'. That is how I got around the city, mostly from the Garrison to New Orleans. I got home about 4.00 o'clock in the afternoon and returned to Camp at midnight.

Many people in New Orleans, by then, were proud of my development, and felt that I was opening for them another path. The respect I received from the boys in the Gap was more pronounced when I started playing for Barbados because many of them with talent had abandoned the game. We had produced one or two very accomplished people in New Orleans, not only in sport, but in other areas. Russell Kellman, for example, became Permanent Secretary in the Ministry of Tourism.

There was also Mrs. Lowe, a midwife in the community, who brought me into the world. This lady used to ride a little bicycle to deliver children all over the city. I was reminded by her when I was maybe 40 years, and had finished playing cricket, that she was very proud of what I had done as a teenager in planning my life around cricket so as to make use of my God given talents. Her comments meant a lot to me, because in New Orleans she was a very upright citizen who placed the welfare of the people above her own, and she was always motivated by service to the community.

The army, then, had rescued me from the clutches of poverty and class oppression in my homeland. I could see no other way to proceed if I wanted to improve my education, maybe see the world, and to play BCA cricket all at the same time. Many doors were closed to me. I was unemployed, or maybe unemployable. My family had much love but not enough latitude to take care of any career dreams that may have been in my head. I was fortunate to have a close knit family that raised me collectively and supported my cricket interests. In the army I entered into another family system that was more than supportive.

All of this, of course, is quite ironic. It was after all an imperial army that had been garrisoned in Barbados for over two hundred years to keep the aggressive foreigners out and the rebellious locals subdued. I had witnessed the workers rebellion in 1937 and knew how quickly the army had moved into position in case events got beyond the competence of the police. But it was war time and it was understood throughout the West Indies that Hitler had to be stopped. It was said in the community that he was killing not only the Jews but the blacks and gypsies. This made it my war, as it was for people like Errol Barrow and all the other men and women who gave service to end what was a horrible assault on humanity. The army provided my first tools of the trade, and from that time I was positioned to master the craft as best I could.

THREE

THE MIND GAME: MASTERING TECHNIQUE AND METHOD

I RECEIVED NO FORMAL COACHING AS A YOUNG PLAYER on my way to national, regional and international status. But I did receive the best possible instruction and guidance from what is now called the 'village academy'. The older folks in the Gap where I lived were severe critics, and did not tolerate any violation of the rules and methods of the game. If a fellow got behind the ball, and used his left shoulder and feet in the right way you would hear that he could bat. If he played across the line, or swiped to mid wicket, he was reprimanded and told to go and learn how to bat. So a chap who could bat, was recognized as disciplined because he was respectful of technique and method.

There was never a shortage of people to show you how to respect methods and techniques. Even men who could not themselves do it in the game were keen advocates of how the youth should begin. It seemed to me that the more a critic was insistent upon these observation the least likely it was that he was any good during his time. But what was sure, and this is also true today, is that a chap need not be an accomplished player in order to be a good coach. In much the same way that a teacher of English grammar need not be an expert novelist, the ability to communicate ways of doing things requires at best a keen eye, good grasp of the issues, and a persuasive way to approach the person being taught.

In each gap of New Orleans there were cricket professors. These were men, and sometimes women, who knew every thing there was to know about the culture of cricket. And they knew all departments of the game. By the time I was eight years old I knew from these experts that cricket is a left sided game for the right hander. If you were a bowler, it was the left hand and left foot, properly coordinated and projected, that gave you the control and the movement, through the air and off the wicket.

The village professors would tell the youngsters to get the 'left hand up in the air', or use that left foot across the width of the crease. You would hear that 'so and so has a good action', and if you were a young prospect this is how you wished to be described. It meant a lot to a chap to hear that he had a good action. You got credit, and the older boys would want to include you in their side, or even allow you to sit in on their cricket conversation. If you had a good action, you qualified to be with adult company.

It was the same with batting. Chest on batsmen were never respected in the village. In fact, you were seen as a kind of abomination unto the Lord. This is how severe the village professors were. You had to get that left shoulder around, elbow out, and view the ball over the left shoulder. The more exaggerated the stance, the more they approved it. A stance was like looking down the barrel of a rifle. That left eyes had to view the object over the left shoulder, and there was no room for deviation. You were allowed to modify your stance within a game in order to deal with a kind of bowler. For example, a good leg spinner might urge you to open your stance a little, but as soon as he was off you were require to return to the norm.

Even young girls would comment that a chap looks 'real good' when he batting, and this was especially rewarding, but what it indicated was that the community had established benchmarks which were known by everyone because cricket was popular culture. It also had a great deal to do with a sense of art because what were upheld were standards of beauty. The people knew of the importance of shape and form. The love of method and technique in the village told me that there were rules in life that should not be broken. I was told that rules were rules and were put in place in order to free the mind to achieve great things and not to inhibit the individual. This took a lot of digesting because as a youth all rules were considered oppressive.

At about ten or so, when my cricket began to take shape, I discovered how rules were liberating rather than oppressive because the more I applied them the greater were my results. It was almost magical when I realized that if I played with a straight bat, driving the ball down the ground, and not swing across, my stumps very rarely got hit. Bowlers found it increasingly difficult to hit my wickets, and I enjoyed the experience of 'staking' out the fellows in the hot sun for hours. With an appreciation of the rules came the mental discipline to apply them relentlessly. Knowing what to do and actually doing it was the difference between the great players and the ordinary ones. I knew this from observation. To watch a great batsman at the crease was like gazing at stars. Some were steady and others were moving. The movement of the eyes, wrist, feet, shoulders, and above all the steadiness of the head, was a high science, and I loved it.

When I entered the BCL I knew all there was to know about the rules, methods and techniques of batting, thanks to the village professors. I was clear on the relationship between method, technique, and performance. All I had to do in the years ahead was to build the discipline and the concentration in order to apply them ruthlessly. It was now left up to me. I was given the rules by the community, and the tools by the army. These were gifts, an investment I could never repay. It was available to all and sundry, and those of us who grasp it with both hands were much the better for it. It was a form of community empowerment that we have taken for granted, but it was the accumulation of decades of knowledge and skill which the elders shared with the youth. I truly was raised to be a cricketer in the New Orleans village academy.

So there was no formal coaching whatsoever. What I also did was to watch very closely the technique and methods of Derek Sealy, who was a master at Combermere School at the time. Sealy had played for the West Indies in the very early years of our Test status. His record was not outstanding but to me he was a very elegant looking player, and I liked that about him. He was beautiful to watch at the crease and, unlike 'Mas George', he did not require the second movement to get into position. He stroke the ball with such effortless ease that you did not notice the very fine movements of the feet. Everything flowed with him, and it was this grace that attracted me and most boys of that time.

There was also Clifford Inniss at Kensington, and George Carew who was an opening batsman for the West Indies. Both had beautiful styles, and were admired as elegant players. These were the people I watched, and I tried to put all of the knowledge I gained from observation into one package. There was a great deal to digest, and back in the Gap the boys would discuss the relative merit of each point made about the different players. Some boys were attracted to the power players whose instinct was to hit the ball out the ground. I was a carpet man, preferring the men who stroke it along the ground. Maybe it was my inner caution, bred from birth. Maybe it was my realization that the rules were the best guide to success.

By the time I got my first opportunity to play under near perfect conditions I was ready. Everything was in place to take full advantage of all I had learnt. I felt like a kid in a candy store. It was on the Kensington Pitch, the closest thing to heaven on earth. The pitch was clean, sweet to look at, level with a shine, a very long way from the wickets on which I had honed my craft. The very first thought that came to my mind, before I took guard, was "how on earth could anyone get out on this?" I was a little ashamed of these feelings but I had never batted on anything like it before. But I knew from my training that I could not abandon my mind and push my hand deep into the cookie jar.

I knew I had to manage my thoughts, to control my reactions. It was a rough transition from pitches that were bouncy with the odd ball 'shooting'. This was not when I played for Barbados. It was during the period when I was a 'fieldhand' at Pickwick, and had an opportunity to get a knock out in the middle. Everything seemed so perfect. The bounce was consistent, distinctly different from what I had experienced on the various pitches in the BCL.

I couldn't believe how such a large gap existed between first class and village venues. The transition in mind was very disturbing because I used to wonder if it was possible to move from my village level to the international level in a short time. Out there in the middle at Kensington I realized that I had received the technical and mental training. But I could not overcome the sensation that it was the most beautiful pitch I had ever seen, and the feeling deep inside that if I got the opportunity to bat on it they would have to drag me off.

The inner confidence I built as a batsman posed a problem for many persons who looked at my small size and assumed that any runs I could possibly make would be in proportion to my height, or something along these lines. I suppose it is true to say that my small size was an influence on my technique, though this was not a matter that occupied my mind. When I went to the crease, for example, my first and foremost thought was not my size but that the ball coming down was not going to get me out.

I was determined that no matter what form I was in, there would be a period of settling in. With this in mind, I decided that the best first posture to adopt was the defensive mode. This was my initial psychological profile. It was as necessary to measure the bowler and see the pitch as it was to get my eyes, legs and hands moving in tandem. It was not fear, if anything it was respect for the game because I learnt very early that if you ill-treated the game it would bite you, and as they say when you get bit by your own dog you are well bitten. Respect was due, and caution was the rule which I applied in my early occupation of the crease.

From the beginning, I developed my batting in such a way as to send the message to bowlers that I was essentially an attacking player. At the same time I understood that the amount of runs I made was in direct relation to my defensive capacity and attitudes. This knowledge came out of the village academy in New Orleans. When a fellow was bowling well, or even hostile, in the case of a pacer, the village professors would shout, "show him the makers name youngster". It was a call for the young batsman to 'ride' the bowler. Villagers got as much pleasure, and sometimes more, from seeing a perfectly executed defensive push, especially against a pacer, as an attacking shot. This was my language because if I had my way I would 'ride' a pacer until it was time to lash him.

I was stimulated by the psychology of the village academy. That I was a little man gave them even more pleasure when I curled up in defense against a hostile pacer. We were taught that when a pacer ran down the wicket in follow through, we should ask him to read the words on the brand label. This is how we respected the role of defense in the building of an innings. This was more important to me than say Clyde whose instinct was to 'pop' the bowler's belt with a cracking drive or to make him take evasive action as the ball flew past his ears.

So this is what I did. I would say to myself, this chap is not going to get me out. The decision was made and implemented immediately because you only have about seven-tenths of a second to do all the thinking. If a chap is bowling at 80-90 miles an hour you don't really have a lot of time to decide where you are going to hit the ball, after deciding that it is not going to get you out. A lot of things could happen in the fleeting moment.

Today I see batsmen pushing forward and committing themselves to the forward stroke before the ball is delivered. I would think, and I am not a mathematician, that if a chap is bowling at 80 miles an hour and you put the front foot out there the ball is going to get to you quicker than if you got on to the back foot. It strikes me also that if you push forward you are getting to the ball quicker, making it even faster than if you were to play back. I don't know the details of the science aspects of this matter, but I would think the longer the ball is in the air the more time you have to watch and play it, especially if you wanted to play your favorite shot.

One of my 'sweet shots' from early days was the extra cover drive, though it was said that the square cut was my signature stroke. To be able to play the extra cover drive requires your eyes, hands, and feet to read from the same page. You played the shot later than the cover drive, and your wrist had to do something that the body was not doing. The man at cover had to be looking to his right while the ball flies to his left. And you had to do this without a significant opening of the foot because if the cover fielder sees that you have opened your foot a little to the left he realizes that you are making room to open the face of the bat. So the extra cover drive is a shot designed to trick the fielders on the off side, and if well played the bowler might feel, momentarily, that he had gotten through.

Then there were the technical aspects of the shot you had to master, and this came from reading the bowler and closely watching the ball. If you are an opening batsman and you want to hit the ball to extra cover while the shine is still on the ball, you aim for mid-off in order to make allowance for the outward movement you should expect. You don't really open the face, because if you do, the ball would go somewhere between point and gully. You should use a firmer bottom hand, allowing the left hand to work as the guide. You should accept that if you have a 'sweet' shot, chances are that you also have a 'sour shot'. It took me some time to admit that my weakness as a batsman was trying to get runs too quickly. If you are too keen to let the bowler know that you are in charge, it could easily degenerate into a weakness. In some cases, of course, it could be both a strength and weakness.

I never had the experience of facing a bowler who had reason to believe that I had a weakness he could exploit. I worked hard at developing scoring shots all around the wicket so as not to rely too heavily on any given shot. I have seen batsmen who were weak on the pads and would make room to cover drive a ball pitched on the middle stump, and that sort of thing. I focused on giving the bowler no grounds to believe in this or that, and to feel therefore that if he got me out he ought to be as surprised as I.

There are two types of weaknesses you can see in a batsman; one is really a flaw, and the other, which has to do with something he loves so much, draws him into a trap. Most humans, I believe, can identify with this latter because it is the cause of most of the problems in the world. Young boys, I know from my coaching years, enjoy playing the on-drive off the back foot because it is the shot of the ballet dancer. You reached up to full height, on the toes, turn, and drive the ball to mid-wicket as it passes the ankle of the right foot.

The trouble with this shot is that you have to open your stance at the last moment to allow the ball to reach deep into the area of the feet. In more cases than not the poor chap would look back to see his stumps fly as he plays over or around the ball. When executed the shot is poetry in motion for sure. Seymour Nurse was a master of this shot which gained him an enormous reputation. But it is always safer to play the shot off the front foot, reaching the ball earlier and hitting it firmly to mid-on rather than later into mid wicket, or just forward of square. The back foot on-drive is more artistic but the front foot version is more dependable.

Many a player had to learn this lesson the painful way before opting for the safer, more productive path. The correct way to play the on-drive is the way it is played by Viv Richards. He played it better than anybody I know, and with so much ease that spectators said for a decade that he was hitting across the line. But Viv would get to the pitch of the ball with a straight bat, and from that position he could hit it nearly any place he wanted.

The Chinese have a proverb which says something to the effect: 'know thyself'. Self- analysis is important because you can learn a lot as a result of reflection. You don't have to beat up on yourself, or become self-obsessed, or anything like that. Just ask yourself a few questions and try to be honest. I used to allow for a lot of reflection, like the grip I was using on the bat, the distance between the bottom hand and the top. In practice I realized that sometimes I played a stroke with too much left hand. I realized that I was looking for placement, and this is not the way to do it. The left hand should be the guiding hand, working to keep the bat straight and balanced while the right hand gives power and placement.

Too many young players today do not understand that it is possible to teach yourself these proper techniques. I often say to them that maybe the earlier players, who had no formal training, watched each other more closely with a view to learn. For instance, I would watch which foot they moved first, the back foot or the front foot. To some bowlers a great player would move the front foot before the back foot and sometimes you move the back foot before the front foot. If you are a keen observer, and a student who wants to master the craft, you would want to know why the different approaches.

If a pacer was bowling 70-80 miles an hour I could readily shift my emphasis to the front foot and eliminate the movement through the air, if he was swinging. Now beyond 85-90 miles you better get back and across, because there is not going to be a lot of movement and you could get into position more readily to play the pull stroke or the cut if it is short, and most bowlers at that pace like to bowl short.

Some batsmen are good enough to play the quickest bowlers through mid-wicket on the front foot. Tom Graveney, for instance, was a tall man who was able to hit even the short-pitch ball in front of mid-wicket. I have noticed that young Kevin Petersen likes to do the same, using his height, and quick eyes, to full advantage. But a shorter man moving back and across, would hook on the back foot behind square.

Older folks in the village believed in the 'back and across' technique, referred to as the English method. We were supposed to be a part of the English batting tradition in which these methods and techniques were developed and perfected. Our village academy, then, was in part a creature of the English tradition. Villagers were expected to perfect the English system in cricket and transfer it to other areas of life, education, religion, politics, and so on. The game was a part of the colonial tutelage we were receiving. The community had not reached that stage in its cricket culture where we were willing to frontally challenge the English technique, either through modification or outright rejection. A few chaps in my time did reject the English method outright, and developed the foundation of a more aggressive, less rules -bound style.

It has been said, for example, that Viv Richards was proud of his declaration of Independence from the Law Lords at Lord's by hitting all and sundry across the line. I have a less extreme interpretation of Viv's method because on close examination it seemed to me that, like 'Mas George'', his bat tended to come down quite straight. He got his left foot to the pitch of the ball. In this regard he was more an orthodox player than he has been given credit for. There is an enormous difference between hitting across the line with a straight bat and doing it with a cross bat. Viv was certainly not a slugger, but a powerful example of what can be done when the left foot gets to the pitch.

In the same vein Gary, with an opened stance, and very little movement at the wicket, was less orthodox. Yet, he played the moving ball with enormous power and precision because of his steady head and quick reflexes. For reasons already mentioned, I was a firm believer in the traditional rules and regulations, and tended to play to the best of my ability within the approved culture.

For some folks in the village, the process of mastering English methods and techniques was a revolution in itself. A working class black boy from the Bridgetown ghetto mastering the methods and techniques of the English aristocracy! I supposed there was something to all of this that should not be taken for granted. I certainly did not see it that way at the time. Yes, we knew that there was an English way of doing things, and for most of us there was no other way, for much the same reason that once we had started to enjoy electoral government we could not imagine a one party state.

What is interesting is how the art and science of the game were transferred from one place to another with such precision and effectiveness. When the mostly Oxford and Cambridge university boys went about the business of globally spreading cricket culture, including a million stories about the achievements of people like W.G. Grace, they could not have imagined that working class children in Kingston, Bridgetown, or Port of Spain, could have mastered and improved upon it.

The learning curve of my generation was steeper than is generally recognized. In 1945, for the West Indies to beat the English at cricket, in England, was considered beyond the imagination. After all you would be beating your master. But some people have a knack of catching on quickly, not only at cricket, but even the English Language, which is a difficult language. I can say quite comfortably that many West Indians handle this language with greater ease than millions of English folk. I wanted to master the English game, and I planned to do so with the tools given me in New Orleans. I was confident on the international stage because the folks in New Orleans were confident in the things they believed in. My BCL apprenticeship was about learning the techniques of the game, including its social aspects, values, competitive culture, and mental application.

I learnt to appreciate the game beyond the boundary; talking to people and listening to different points of view. I was not generally a great contributor but I was a generous listener. As a teenager I spent a lot of time with men within the 24 and 30 age group. I would listen to what they were saying, and how they were saying it. You had to be sharp enough to grasp the subtle use of words in their speech. Very rarely would they speak directly. The twist in the speech would say everything. Some of it I never digested, but most of it I spent a lot of time thinking about.

There was a chap called Gerald, for example, who was senior to me, but we played together; he was a left arm spinner. I had not seen one better until I saw Alf Valentine. This chap really spun the ball. You could hear it whistling when he delivered. I wanted to know how he did this because I fancied myself as a useful off-spinner. I would tag along to pick up tips and to read his mind. It was an amazing gift he had, but there was no set up in those days to expose a chap like that. He would have done very well at any level of the game.

I also enjoyed being around Fred Howard, a tennis star who played cricket. He had an excellent grasp of the dynamics of a moving ball. Fred was a scientist before the age of science in sports. We were fascinated by how he spoke. Today we hear about bio-mechanic in sports and so on, but Fred would speak clearly about the moving ball, the way muscles worked, and how to avoid injury while pushing the body to the full. He coached tennis players in Belleville and such like elite communities. He could not play tennis for Barbados but he coached the people who did.

The performance quality of BCL cricket was high. There was a chap called Agard, a seaman, who played for one of the clubs. There was also Matthews, a ripping off-spinner who played only on Thursdays because he was a Seventh-Day Adventist. Recently, I was pleased to hear other people confirm my observation that in a more democratic time both would have had a good chance of being West Indies players.

The vision Mitchie Hewitt had for the BCL took us on board and opened the door for a few, but there were many others who were excluded. For me he is a national hero and his name should have been in the discussion when Parliament declared the official pantheon. This gentleman did so much for cricket, for the masses of people, and for the organized game. I see him as a great liberator.

When Hewitt took over the leadership of the BCL structure, and started collecting fees to fund an expansion program, clubs began springing up everywhere. Literally everywhere! We had something like 80 clubs at one stage. The unfortunate aspect of the competition in retrospect was that players who were not selected for their team would walk away, and form another club. In this way a lot of the clubs sprang up, and the BCL became associated with a general lack of effective governance.

I stayed with Westshire for all my BCL years. Well, I couldn't think of joining another club because my cousin used to pay my fees. It was something like a penny a week to be a member of the club. Not only that, we had a membership of 16 or so, and as the youngest in the club I naturally saw an opportunity to play in every game. Matches began at 2pm and went until sundown. We played on Thursdays because most workers got half day from work on that day. It was knock-out cricket, but played over two days. Sometimes the two teams would arrive in order to prepare the pitch because there was no groundsman. We played mostly around the city-Beckles Road, Carrington's Village, Black Rock, and Spooners Hill. But we knew that there were good players in St. Andrew, St. Lucy, St Philip, and other rural parts who were playing excellent cricket.

Mr. Hewitt would see to it that scores were published in the press. If I got a few runs my family would have an interest in buying a newspaper, but in those days funds were very tight and word of mouth had to suffice. I remember getting a few runs off Ormond Graham, who played eventually for Barbados. He was a quick bowler, and on rough pitches was quite dangerous. It seemed to me that he was bowling 150 miles an

49

hour. Charlie Graham, Ormond's brother, was keeping wicket, and I remember him coming up to the stumps and saying something like "don't back away, son, you are too good a player to back away". He was one of the several people who helped me at that stage in the transition.

The more I played the better my technique became. Clyde had a reputation even then as a hard hitter. I never played with him, though he lived just around the corner from my home. I played with Frank and we had a little competition going- the Bank Hall boys versus the Westbury Road boys. We played at a place called 'The Burn House', just up the street by the Empire Club. On Saturday mornings we had these fun matches that later included teams from Eagle Hall, Black Rock, and Bank Hall. We were friends at a very early age. We didn't see a lot of each other because he lived a mile away, and at 11 years old in those days a mile was a long way to visit friends. But I had a lot of admiration for him because he was playing for Combermere, and doing very well.

Frank, Clyde and I arrived as teammates at the national level through different routes. I came through the BCL, and they through the BCA. I would see Clyde occasionally in the verandah of his home on Baxter's Road where he was born. But people were already saying that as youngsters we had potential to go all the way. Clyde was a promising cricketer, a good footballer, and an impressive athlete. Keith, his brother, was also a good cricketer, and a respected footballer. Unfortunately, he developed eye problems early in life. They played in the backyard of their home. I played in the gaps of my community.

It is fair to say that by the age of 15 we knew pretty much all of the technical requirements to be good players. It was for us to apply this knowledge as we moved through different levels of the game. We had to deal with a lot of changes over a short period of time. Sometimes I came up against a new situation that boosted my confidence. For instance, when I was playing in the Army we had a chap name Jim Parris, a leg spin bowler who had played for Barbados back in 1935, and who had gone to the War. When he came back he bowled at me in practice at the Garrison, and wanted to know more about the little fellow who could read his googly. By then I was playing cricket for Barbados. Many people had problems reading his googly because he spun the ball viciously. His length and direction were not always the best, and he was rather surprised that I could pick him.

It was exciting hearing his accounts of the war. I was in the army, and for me it was a job, my first ever real employment. The War had brought an end to international Test cricket, and the West Indies did not play again until 1948, even though the War had finished in 1942. I followed news of the 1939 tour because Headley was my champion player and I was keen to know of his contributions. In the first Test at Lords he scored 106 and 107. He was the only West Indian, apart from my namesake K.H. Weekes, who got 137 in the third Test at the Oval, to show international class. The next tour to the West Indies was the one in which I made my debut, against England at Kensington Oval on January 21, 1948. Headley also played in that Test, batting at no. 5, two spots below me.

From the Garrison Sports Club I was selected for the Barbados team in 1945. My selection was considered an investment in a young player. I had to perform at the Garrison, and I did. In fact I was doing pretty well. We won the BCA competition in 1947. I scored my first century in the BCA against the Police at the Garrison. I was 19 years old. Finally, I was playing on well prepared pitches. I was ready to apply my BCL experience and cricket knowledge from the New Orleans village academy.

FOUR

BEATING BCA BALL:
THE SOLDIER INSIDE

GOOD FORTUNE SMILED, and my first century in the BCA was a double. The significance is testament that my reading and assessment of the transition from the BCL to BCA was accurate. I had arrived at the opinion that once placed in a situation where the facilities, field and pitch, were developed, I would apply what I had learnt in the BCL and the village academy to beneficial effect. By 19, my ability to concentrate, and to manage my thoughts, was showing returns on the investment of time and energy. This was the basis of the first effort at making big scores. It did not come naturally, though my character disposed me in a direction where thinking about issues around me was the norm.

In those days you scored centuries if you wanted to be taken seriously as a batsman. The mental approach to scoring centuries is as vital as you can imagine, and teenagers back then scored centuries regularly. We knew how to 'ride' big bowlers, and how to punish them when they slip. There was a toughness involved, and if you had ability you would show this toughness before you were eighteen.

After scoring the double century against the Police, I was called to trials for Barbados. I began the trials by scoring a century, and continued making big scores until I got into the Barbados team. The wickets were good, and I was prepared mentally, emotionally, and physically for the contest. I knew that it was important for me to out-perform the competition, coming from the Gap with no impressive references from school or business. All I had was what was given me in New Orleans, and that was an appetite for runs and the skills to satisfy the thirst. Maybe that is all you need. When you are out there in the middle nothing else counts. You cannot say to a bowler, look here chap, do you know where I went to school? Do you know who my father is? You could, but in those days that would be like waving a red rag in front of a bull.

The art and science of batting are about the dialogue between the body and the 'inner man'. My insides were built upon the foundations of the earliest BCL vision. The mission of the League was to show that in the villages of the island there was a lot of intellectual ammunition with which to build Barbados and West Indies cricket. I went to the crease as an ambassador of the villages. I was in the BCA but I was from the BCL, and I wanted that much understood. It was important to me that those I played with understood this because the crowds that watched the games knew that was where I came from. I was the underdog, so to speak, coming from below, even though I was playing at the highest national level.

The cricket was tough in the BCA. High standards were built into the competition, and the leading clubs were proud of their legacies, and looked after their players. There was a lot of discipline and respect within the competition, and crowds came out to watch 'hot, steamy' cricket played in good spirit. Some games were more competitive than Test matches I played. Players did it for pride and were not prepared to give anything away. If you were a rookie, you needed the help of the Almighty because they came at you with everything they had, including the experience which you lacked.

If you wanted recognition, you had to perform, and do so consistently because one century could easily land you the nickname 'flash in the pan', or 'one shot Willie'. You had to perform with persistence because there was a lot of aggression in the competition. I came along with brilliant young players such as Frank and Clyde, Johnnie Lucas, 'Bricky' Lucas, Proverbs from Wanderers, the Marshall boys, and Denis Atkinson, to name a few. If you wanted to keep that kind of company you could not fall short of the mark. If you were a batsman, you had to prove it with centuries, as simple as that. And you had to score good looking centuries.

A good looking century was a work of art. It had to be played with toughness and flare. You had to show that you could stick in the "fellows' throat like a fishbone", and be prepared to 'cut their tail like a school master'. Not too many fancy shot were required, but occasionally you showed that you had them and could pull them out of the draw at any time. But, critically, you could not be 'edging the peoples' ball.' And if you played a cover drive through fine leg you were dead in the water because the people would talk about it for years to come. You would hear things like, "Oh, you are the chap who broke down fine leg with cover drives?" And they would ask you this question at very impolite times, like when you were talking to a lady of choice.

The BCA at this time was filled with some very young players, many still in their teens. We felt that we were big men; maybe we were socially a little more mature than youngsters today, though not as well educated and informed. We probably had a little more social knowledge and wisdom, but not the racial courage of the youth today. I was not keen on the party scene, though I did not run away from meaningful discussion with the ladies, and took in a little of the night life. I went to the 'Little Hops", the dances were called then. A group of us from the army would go to the "hops" and dance to the sound of the big band – Glen Miller, the Duke, and Count Basie. There were also a few good local bands, and some of them were just getting ready to break away from American music and develop something that was Barbadian.

We also went to dances at Queen's Park and the Garrison. The Empire Cricket Club held a fund-raising dance at the Garrison every Christmas night. Spartan Cricket Club had a dance on Old Years night. The various cricket clubs would have dances at different times, for fund raising, birthday celebrations, and so on. People would have their private dances at Queen's Park, and these were big attractions. But in general, my difficulty was that you would meet the same people everywhere, and the same selection of girls with whom to dance. We were big dancers, especially Clyde and Frank. We enjoyed the experience, the fancy footwork, and the graceful movement across the floor. Dancing for us was an extension of the footwork and coordination required to be a good batsman. The rhythm, the balance, and the quick movement of body parts, were the common ingredients of good batting and good dancing.

Dancing was a part of my mental and physical training, and we understood this as teenagers. Getting the feet nimble, light and prepared for flight, was a part of the athleticism that cricket required. The village professors did not give a chap any marks for planting his feet in the crease like a mahogany tree. A flat footed batsman was the last thing the crowd wanted to see. You would hear the crowd shouting, "wait, he is a sheep or what? Who tied he to a stake?; Somebody, please untie that boy and let he go home to he mudda". I remember once, some years ago, watching a match in which Wayne Daniel, the fast bowler, was frequently over-stepping the crease. After the game a chap came up to me and said, 'these young fellows need to get back into ballroom dancing; his rhythm and balance are off'".

The Garrison Sports Club produced strong teams, and was a good launch pad for many careers. The whole team effort was based on the discipline of each member. We were a disciplined group of people. That was part of the training. At 6.00 am we reported to the parade ground. The routine was good for the strengthening of mind and body. Excuses were not a part of the training. There were not many stars in the side, but it was a strong team that relied on each player looking out for the others. Not many of them played for Barbados, but we were able to win the BCA competition. It was here that I fully understood the notion that the magnificence of the whole is greater than the sum of the parts.

My place in the batting order varied between three and four. I had no fixed position; it all depended on the balance of the team and the state of the match. I was happy in either position, and never indicated a preference. In the early days I preferred, however, to field at cover; I liked being busy, and the cover position was a coveted location for chaps who were fit and quick on the ground. It was a specialist position, and youngsters used to compete to patrol the cover area. It brought honour to be described as a good cover, and to be able to read a batsman's hands so as not to be thrown off side was a skill.

In the village you were expected to be an all rounder simply because you had to take a wicket in order to bat. That is how we played in the Gap. You would have several bowlers and the one who takes the wicket had the right to bat. That was one type of game we played in order to encourage all the boys to bowl. You had to work for your supper. A good bowler would bat more often than the rest. If we had more players than bowlers, we adjusted the rules so that the chap who takes a catch got the right to bat. In this version, the bowler was under pressure to hit the wickets. I came through this tradition, and fancied myself as a little spinner.

I bowled off and leg breaks. I wouldn't say that I was a spinner in the true sense of the term. I was a slow bowler who did a little something with the ball. The word got out that I gave it a tweet, a rumor spread by batsmen. Let's face it, a batsman would have an interest in saying that the ball which got him out turned square. I never denied the charge, and sometimes I would ride on this reputation. In the Garrison teams we had genuine spinners like Callendar, Bertie's father, who did wonders with his left arm; we also had Parris who was reliable and effective.

The officers did not play cricket in the team. A few of them played football. Captain Chase, for example, was a good footballer, so too was Major Warren. We didn't have any white players, and most of the officers were English. When I became established in the team it did not occur to me that I should leave and join another club. The concept of team loyalty was so embedded in my mind I would not have migrated to another club if a good offer was made. I received an invitation to join Empire. No one from Spartan, the club of the black career professionals, invited me. The late Harold Griffith, son of the founder, Herman Griffith, invited me to play for Empire. He and the late Charles Alleyne, my long time buddy, invited me to move over to Empire while I was at the Garrison Sports Club. As much as I liked the Empire boys, and respected the club, I had a deep commitment to the army and could not accept.

At the time I was not thinking about a long term career in the Army. My mind was still locked into self improvement in order to become a civil servant. This was the path to security and respectability. It was the main path for my contemporaries who had received a secondary education. Ex-cricketers became civil servants. It was a place where, as a government employee, benefits could be had for your family well beyond retirement. I was keeping company with people like Charles Alleyne, Frank Taylor, Ashley Drayton and one or two other members of Empire Club. All of them were civil servants, and to me they appeared very comfortable. This was a dream for boys with my background; security, respect, and material comfort.

But then good fortune struck once again and I was invited to make my debut for Barbados against England in the 1947/48 home series. I was still in the century scoring mode. As I said, in those days you had to be into the business of scoring centuries. It had to be a way of life. You had to score centuries for the love of it and because you loved it. People had to know you as the chap who likes scoring centuries. But you could not become a century maker, as a way of life, unless you had put in place the life style to enable it. The discipline, fitness, self-control, strategic thinking, and respect for the rules and culture of the game. When the door opened to play against England, my first international engagement, I was ready in mind and body.

I stepped into the international game as I had entered the BCA; by scoring a century. Again, I was proving to myself that the key to success was hard work and effective mental preparation. England was a strong team. They came out with Jim Laker, the mystery spinner who ran riot through the West Indies team. The hundred against England sent a few shivers down some spines because shortly thereafter I received a cable from a club in England inviting me to play as a professional in the Lancashire League. There were quite a few players in the England team from Lancashire. The word went back that a little fellow from Barbados had just done something interesting, and that he would light up the grey grounds in the League. The Leagues in England were at the stage where they were recruiting West Indian professionals. Learie Constantine had established throughout the country the attractiveness of the West Indian brand of cricket. The crowds appreciated it, and wanted more. But I did not accept. I was not ready.

I was still thinking about how best to establish my credentials in Barbados as a leading batsman. There were some outstanding matters, mostly psychological, about the way I was selected for Barbados that needed to be settled. I did not receive a cable, and no one came to knock on my door. Other players from a more privileged background received formal communications in the way befitting the nature of the assignment. It was 1945, and I was selected to represent Barbados against Trinidad at Queens Park Oval.

60

I heard about my selection in the street, and then on the Rediffusion. It was a feeling that could never be properly described. The honour and privilege of representing your country is beyond calculation, and especially for me coming from the BCL. I wished that there had been a letter, something tangible I could have shown my mother, something to keep. But that was not to be. The public wire was the medium. When I heard it I was in camp; in fact I was on a training course in the parish of St. Andrew. I was brought from St. Andrew and given leave to go and practice with the other members of the Barbados team.

I was the last of the 3Ws to make my debut for Barbados. Clyde played in early January 1942 and scored 8 and 0 in his first match which was also against Trinidad. In my debut in 1945 I did exactly the same, scored 0 and 8. Frank also had his debut against Trinidad, which he did in January 1942, scoring 29 and 6. So we were all off to poor starts in the regional competition. Our captain, Tom Pierce, a fine gentleman, was very encouraging. It was not long before we climbed the ladder and got on top of the regional game.

Clyde struck 70 in his second game and 67 in his third, and two years later struck his first regional century, 125 against Guiana in October 1944. Frank was first out the blocks with 188 against Trinidad in Port of Spain in February 1943, and then came the first of the two historic slaughters of Trinidad in February 1944; Frank 308 not out. Clyde continued his assault on regional bowlers. After his 125 against British Guiana at Bourda in October 1944, he followed with 103 against Trinidad in February 1945.

It was a very tall order to look up to. I entered the Barbados side batting at no. 6, with Clyde at 3, and Frank at 4. Clyde's total of 4 in the first innings was followed by 103 in the second, and Frank's struck 74 and 61 while I could only muster 0 and 8. In my second match I scored 53 while Frank got 113. Clyde followed Frank with a triple against Trinidad in the second of the two historic slaughters in February 1946 at Queen's Park Oval, an innings that Frank was to watch from the other end. When captain Peirce declared at 619 for 3, Clyde was 314 not out and Frank 255 not out.

It was not until September the following year that I joined the century club, scoring 129 against British Guiana at Bourda, a match in which neither Frank nor Clyde played, but in which there were two other centuries, John Goddard, the captain, 114 and A.M.Taylor, 110 not out batting at no. 9. After a score of 97 against Jamaica in March 1947 at Melbourne Park in Kingston, a match in which my hero 'Mas George', one year short of 40, scored 203 not out and 57 not out. I scored another century the following week at Sabina Park, a patient 123 batting at no. 4, sandwiched between Clyde at 3 and Frank at 4. It was not until February 1950 that I got my first regional double, 236 not out against British Guiana at Kensington Oval.

During this period we had no sense that we would have emerged as what some pundits described, the greatest middle order in the history of Test cricket. We knew we were doing well and as individuals we were getting on top of our game. But the concept of the 3Ws had not yet evolved. It was not until 1950 in England that the term began to be used widely, which served our purpose because if one failed or even two and the other did well it was still the 3Ws that saved the day. Being one unit made it comforting because there was a good chance that one of us would get some runs and take the pressure off the other two. So we were happy with the merger. It made good business sense, as the financial analysts would say.

In 1950 on the English tour we played cricket six days a week. We were getting runs and the radio men, then the print men, the journalists who followed the tour, began to carry stories about the 3Ws. Before we knew what was happening, the whole world had caught on, and as they say, the rest is history. The label stuck. At first it was kind of cute but later the gravity of the matter struck. We were at the heart of West Indies batting.

There was an enormous expectation. We were to ensure that West Indian batting reach the international level and stayed there. There was much pride and at the same time it was an enormous honour and weight. It was the first time that such a system had been put in place. We were to consolidate the batting department, and we had found two excellent spinners in Ramadhin and Valentine. We were looking like a very competitive international outfit.

This was a major development for us. We knew we were a part of something enormous. The West Indies team never really had a reliable batting line-up, not since we had gained Test status in 1927 and played our first series in 1928, losing 3-0 against England. During the 1930s 'Mas George' carried the batting. It was a one man show, to a large extent. They were some fine batsmen in the team, but they never really came together as a competitive unit.

Headley scored the bulk of the runs. When he failed we were out to sea. When he got runs we were in with a chance. That was the Headley reality; we knew about it. This is why he was my hero, not only because he was a great batsman, but because he made us proud by carrying the burden of our batting for some twenty years, giving us some measure of respectability as a Test team. Without him we would have been nothing to be taken seriously. We knew, as the 3Ws, that he had passed the baton to us.

The record of Headleys performance is really quite remarkable. He made his debut in Barbados against England on the 1930 tour of the West Indies. The first match was drawn, and this was largely because of the 176 he made from a second innings total of 384. England won the second Test at Queens Park Oval; Headley failed, scoring 8 and 39. In the third Test at Bourda, Headley scored 114 and 112 and the West Indies won their first Test match after six attempts. In the third Test at Sabina Park, the game was drawn because Headley scored a massive 223, after England had amassed a first innings total of 849. This was the game in which A. Sandham established the Test record of 325 runs.

The following year we went off to Australia where we lost the series 4-1. It was a slaughter, losing three Tests by an innings. Headley became the first West Indian batsman to score a century against the Aussies. Three centuries were scored by the West Indies on the tour and Headley made two of them, the other was made by F.R. Martin, an excellent 123 not out while opening the batting. West Indies won the last Test because of this innings which was played with Headley who scored 105.

Then we went off to England in 1933. Headley scored 13 and 50 in the first Test and we lost by an innings. In the second Test he scored 169 and we were able to draw the match. In the third Test Headley failed, and we were defeated by an innings. England returned to the West Indies in 1935. We lost the first Test, though Headley made the highest score by any West Indies batsman, 44 run out. West Indies won the second Test. Headley made 93, the highest score of the match. The third Test was rain affected and drawn, while West Indies won the 4th Test at Sabina Park because Headley scored an imposing 270.

The West Indies returned to England in 1939. The hosts won the first Test despite scores of 106 and 107 from Headley. The team was able to score a modest 277 and 225. The second Test was rain affected and came to a tame draw, as was the fourth in which K.H .Weekes scored 137 and Headley 65 run out.

This was the legacy we were asked to carry. The three of us made our Test debut in the post war Test series of 1948. Headley had missed nearly ten years of Test cricket, a crime if ever there was one. He returned in the 1948 series, aged and not in the best of fitness. In the first Test I batted at no. 3 and he at no. 5, scoring 35 and 29 respectively in the first innings. He did not play in the second Test in which yours truly, Frank and Clyde scored 36, 97 and 20 respectively in the first innings. In the third Test Clyde scored 11 and Frank 131. I made 36, We saw the West Indies to victory in British Guiana. In the 4th Test at Sabina Park we won again with yours truly scoring 141, Frank 38 and Clyde 45.

It was always a great pleasure batting with Frank and Clyde. It was easier to get runs batting with Clyde because Frank's style was rather similar to my own. Sometimes the field placing, because of Clyde ability to hit hard to mid-off and mid-on, and over extra cover, allowed me to take advantage of openings. I scored a lot of runs playing squarish on both sides, but Clyde was more aggressive in using the 'V' down the wicket. In those days captains would not move the field around each time the strike rotated, so I took advantage of the open space. When I say that Clyde was a power player, you have to understand that this is no overstatement. He would hit the ball straight, and very hard. Sometimes the non-striker, the umpire, and most of all the bowler in his follow through were in big trouble. Frank was more like Lara, maybe slightly more delicate. He would push the ball with perfect timing pass mid-off and extra cover.

I felt comfortable with Frank and Clyde, secure in a way because in those early days scoring runs was no guarantee of selection. There were always a lot of off the field issues that could determine selection. It took me a little time to feel secure in the Barbados and West Indies teams. There were the issues of race and class that dominated the social world of cricket. Everyone who was honest would admit this, but very few people were prepared to talk about it, or to try to eradicate its power.

It was very strong in Barbados but also in Jamaica. George Headley had his troubles in the early days. He did not discuss it much but he was very aware of the nature of these things. Prior to my Test debut in 1948 a black man had never captained the West Indies side. White players like the Grant brothers from Trinidad captained Headley, men who could not try on his cricket boots.

Headley captained just one Test, the one in which I made my West Indies debut in January 1948. It was a one-off game, but during the 1930s when he carried the team on his back he was considered too black and too poor and without an appropriate education. The prejudice was very intense. I was never captained by a black man in the Barbados team. When I became captain in 1960 I was the first long term black to lead Barbados.

This was the racial environment in which I grew up as a national and international cricketer. It was ruled by strong racist principles and a chap, especially one like me from the working class, had to be very careful. It was not that I was sensitive, or had a chip on my shoulder. This was the hard reality that shaped Barbados and Caribbean society. I supposed it was the same in most institutions.

Trinidad, on the other hand, was accustomed to having a multi-racial sporting culture. There Blacks, Indians, Whites, Chinese, Jews, Syrians, and mixed race groups, played in the same teams, and had been doing so since the end of the 19th century. In Barbados the cricket team was dominated by the professional and property owning classes. I was a bit of an odd ball in that sense, and for some people I was the rabbit that came out the hole and ran across the field. I am not sure if there was any celebration around my selection in New Orleans. If there was, I was not invited. But the community was not surprised. It had grown to have confidence in my ability and commitment to the excellence for which it stood.

It was in the army that there was a festive mood around my selection. The Army had given me the gift of an open door, and provided me with gear to ensure that I looked the part. I cannot overstate the contribution it made to my life and development as a person. I took the opportunity to do a fair amount of reading, and well remember the classes conducted by Sir Clyde Gollop. I was made a local acting [unpaid] Lance Corporal, a status designed to protect me from some of the more menial duties new recruits were expected to perform. I became Lance Corporal Weekes, 6752.

This did not go down well with everyone. Some of the boys in the camp said that I was made Lance Corporal because I played cricket and football. But this was not true because we all sat an exam and I did fairly well, I was told. Eventually, I did a little teaching, offering instructions to new recruits and that sort of thing. Sometimes when I was offering instructions on the texts recruits were asked to study for the class, I could hear some of the chaps saying, 'he sounds like he is a real Lance Corporal; he knows the stuff'. I was getting the feeling of being an army man, and it was very pleasing. In time I got the respect from those fellows who were skeptics. I felt that I had won a few battles on both fronts; in the tough world of army business and on the field of play.

FIVE

STORMING KENSINGTON: REPRESENTING BARBADOS

I HAD TWO CAPTAINS IN MY EARLY DAYS as a Barbados player; Tom Pierce and John Goddard. There were very different types of characters and our relations varied. They handled the Barbados team in unique ways that reflected their personalities. My first captain, Pierce, was not as good a cricketer as Goddard, but he was very knowledgeable and compassionate. I would say his approach and attitude to players reflected that he knew more than a little about cricket. I am not going to speak about the opinions of Frank and Clyde but I will say that to the best of my memory he was highly respectful of us and we in turn of him.

John Goddard was closer to us in age, and was a rugged, business-like sort of person. He played the game hard, and he was respected as a good player. Tom never thought he was as good as most of the other players in the side. But because of his humility and general demeanour he received a lot more respect. Goddard was respected but he was not the type of person who would sit down with players over a beer and go through an inning after a day's play. He would come into the dressing room, say what he had to say, and off he went. Tom would sit back and talk with us about what transpired. This would happen every day. They were both white Barbadians, but possessed very different types of personalities.

Goddard was part of the Barbados merchant class. Pierce was a professional man, in the insurance business. He played at Wanderers while Goddard was a Pickwick man. I did not notice at the time, but I was told later that the divide between Pickwick and Wanderers was deep and sometimes became bitter. They were different types of clubs, representing different classes, like Spartan and Empire. Herman Griffith was blackballed a few times trying to join Spartan, and eventually rejected it and formed his own club, Empire. Later, many black people in turn had problems getting into the Empire Club. If Herman though you were a good black boy he would welcome you to come and join the Empire Club. He was looking for a classy sort of black person, because he was very much up against the respectability of Spartan and the brown skin boys.

But these two captains, Goddard and Pierce, had an enormous influence over the Barbados team, both in terms of selection, and in shaping the future of players. They were friends and got along very well. Pierce captained Goddard as well, and participated in the decision to select Goddard as captain. Herman Griffith captained Barbados in 1941 for a few matches, the first black man to do so. It was a token of appreciation for services to Barbados and West Indies cricket.

The task of Pierce and later Goddard was to heal the wounds that existed in Barbados club cricket, and to forge a national team. This was not an easy task because the competition between clubs in those days was pretty rough; it was almost tribal in term of passions and turf rule. You had players from Spartan, Empire, Pickwick, and Wanderers who saw each other in domestic cricket as the enemy. But they had to put that behind them and play as a unified Barbados team. This was a serious matter because the pride of club was stronger than the pride of country. We had no developed sense of nation in those colonial days. There was no democracy and self government. We were managed from London and this did not encourage a sense of ownership in our public institutions. The clubs produced factions that were very real within the Barbados team.

The other clubs did not produce enough players to influence relations within the team. I was not a clique man because I came from the BCL and the Army, and neither had a tradition of privilege in Barbados cricket. Then there were the schoolboys, like Frank and Clyde who came into the Barbados side without strong club loyalties, other than to their school, Combermere and Harrison's respectively. As an outsider it was very important for me to read and comprehend these groupings that carried strong sentiments and emotional bonds. You had to be very careful because you did not always know where a fellow stood in relation to these cleavages that were influential on and off the field.

Pierce was a selector in those days, and exercised this right by virtue of being the captain. He was very keen on ensuring that the players were respected and well treated. We appreciated that because we were young and unsure about a lot of things in the official world. We did not get a blazer and tie by virtue of playing for our country. There was none of that initially, and I was particularly concerned about it because I was not long in my pocket.

I was told of my selection, and that it was entirely up to me to outfit myself. I would have been in great difficulty had I not been outfitted by the Army- the Garrison's Sports Club. If a chap in my circumstance had no sponsor it was likely he would have missed the tour. It is also possible that he might not have been selected in the first instance. Few players, if any, were selected who were not self-reliant. I was the only one who could not have helped himself, and maybe Frank, although his parents were overseas and might have helped. The Army made sure that I had clothing, boots and batting equipment.

There was no active talent scouting program among the BCL. This policy did not change until the late 50s and early 60s. Prior to that cricket conversations focused on the old clubs and the school tie. I would hear from time to time that I was the one that got away. Becoming a Barbadian player did not change my life in any significant material way. For sure it added a sense of importance, the status of being a national representative. The social impact was also minimal because I kept the same company, and moved about society in more or less the same way. I spent more time with Frank than before. We were good buddies from childhood. Neither of us had any reason to believe that we would have made the Barbados side at a young age, and when we did it came as a surprise to us and many people. I was very influenced by Frank because he got his opportunity before I did, and he was very encouraging. He was more convinced than I about my chances, and he did his best to talk me into looking in that direction.

But my social life underwent no significant adjustment. I was not comfortable with a lot of what was happening around me, and I preferred to keep away from certain people and places. In any event I was happy with my friends and more comfortable with my community. It was sometimes difficult to explain why I refused invitations to do certain things and go some places. But I was very keen on maintaining my integrity. My philosophy was simple: if you did not consider me a worthwhile person before I played for Barbados it was unlikely that I would consider your company special to me in any way.

I did try to use what little influence I had as a Barbados player to open doors for youngsters in much the same way that I had benefited. Whenever I was in a position, I would go to New Orleans in order to see if I could bring along a young player. I practiced this policy during my Test years, and into my retirement when I became the Government cricket coach. I tried really hard to get the BCL players exposed. But I still had to cope with hindrances from the chaps sitting next to me as a selector and asking silly questions like 'where does he come from?' I did not know why the social origins of a player should matter if he was producing performances as a cricketer. But I experienced quite a bit of that. It took a lot of doing to change such attitude among some people, and I am not sure that it is now behind us.

I was paid a stipend rather than a salary as a Barbados player. It remained difficult for me to live as a national player because I had no profession, no property, and no high school certification. I received 30 dollars a match. It was not possible to live on this. I do not think it was the expectation that a cricketer should live on this stipend. This was meant to cover pocket expenses; all the other players had regular incomes. I was getting a small salary in the Army which held me together. When I was discharged in 1947 all this was to change quite drastically.

After my selection for Barbados to play against England in the 1947/8 series, a few opportunities appeared, and I was in a better position to make decision about my future. The financial stress I experienced was not the worst. I still lived at home in those years. I did not leave my mother's home in New Orleans until 1955 when I was close to retirement from Test cricket. By then I was married and had built a home. In the end I shared two homes, one with my mother, and the other with my wife.

I enjoyed touring the Caribbean in the regional competition. It was the first time I traveled the region; and quite an eye opening experience it was. I was fascinated by the variations in Caribbean culture, language and landscape. Trinidad was in sharp contrast to Barbados in terms of the diversity of populations and the openness of the society. Jamaica was striking in terms of its physical beauty, the energy and hospitality of the people. I was probably more outgoing in these islands than at home, the reason being that there was a great deal of new things to discover.

In 1946 we went to British Guiana. Frank and Clyde were not with us. They went to New York to play exhibition cricket to earn a few dollars. British Guiana was an extraordinary experience. I was in awe of the massive, intimidating landscape, with rivers that contained islands bigger than Barbados. From there we traveled to Jamaica that has remained a favorite. If you were a well known person and you wished to get away from the crowd, Jamaica was a wonderful place to be. I enjoyed the countryside, the fairness of the people, and the excellent food.

The Jamaicans thought I batted more like George Headley than any other West Indian player, and eventually gave me a warm reception. Maybe it was our small size that endeared us to a people who have a history of standing up for the underdog. But we had very different styles. They knew that George was my hero. I had made this clear on a number of occasions, but then again he was everyone's hero.

I stuck pretty close to George. Wherever he went I was clinging to him. I enjoyed his company and thought he was one of the finest gentlemen I had ever met. I was impressed with his easy, firm and clear style of speaking. He spoke with precision, and no rancour. He would tell the harsh truth in a dignified sort of way. For me he was a role model in more ways than one. He was precise with words, and there was never a questioning of his clarity. He had the wisdom of a philosopher.

It was a learning period for me. I was proud to sit back and talk cricket with George. He was very generous with his knowledge. He would tell us little things that we would never forget. In my first match against Jamaica at Melbourne Park in Kingston in March 1947, I was batting quite well, cruising to a century. Headley used to bowl some little off breaks, and on 97 in the first innings I went cutting at one that did a little and edged to the keeper, G.H. Mudie. Headley picked up four for 40 in that innings. Later in the evening he called me over and said, 'Everton, you should never cut in the '90s'. Well, I never forgot that piece of advice. In the 1950 West Indies tour of England I was on 290 in a match, played the cut stroke and missed. Apparently, in admonishing myself, I said loudly 'don't cut in the nineties.' The wicketkeeper, a South African, took the opportunity of a cocktail party that evening to tell the gathering that a batsman should never cut in the nineties. He ended by saying, 'imagine this, my aggregate for the entire season is less than 290, and Everton is chastising himself for cutting in the nineties.'

It was said that George and I found common ground and bonded because of our similar background and social experiences. He was the product of a working class family. He came through the cricket system that was fostered by the sugar estates in the parish of St. Catherine. We got along beautifully, and did a lot of things together. In 1950 he substituted for me as professional in Bacup, the Lancashire League team to which I was contracted. He went there for a season. By then, of course, he was not in the best of fitness, even though he played for the West Indies as late as in 1954 at the age of 43.

The contrast in terms of my relationship with players like Goddard was striking. He was a fine player but we had nothing in common in terms of social understanding. We played cricket for our country and region, but we had different philosophies about how our society should develop, and the nature of race relations. He was a part of the Barbados elite system that had conspired to keep people like me in the margins. I did not hold these things against anyone personally. It was a system from the past that we inherited. Some people benefited from it and tried to preserve it. Those of us who suffered from it wanted it changed. In such a circumstance relations would have been a little tense.

Goddard could have made the Barbados team as a bowler or batsman, and he was one of the finest fielders in the country. He was a part of that long tradition of elite white players who had done a great deal to build the foundations of Barbados and West Indies cricket. There is no doubt that they did a magnificent job in setting up West Indies cricket as a system with clubs and institutional support. But they built it for themselves and by seeking to exclude others from positions of honour we ended up with cricket being a place where a race and class war was being waged.

Further, Goddard was in the tradition of distinguished players from Barbados who made the West Indies team, persons like the great George Challenor, H.G.B Austin, and E.L.G Hoad. He bowled quick off-spinners, and was a good seamer as well, though in the latter mode some said that his action was a little suspect. While he was not willing to have an intimate conversation with his black players about the game, their futures and careers, and appeared aloof and indifferent, he was a class player who served Barbados and West Indies cricket well.

Politics was always at the centre of Barbados cricket. Few players, however, got involved in the deep end of party politics. During the 1940s the radical labour politics of Sir Grantley Adams and Wynter Crawford was in full stride and we were all keen to see how it would have its impact on the culture of cricket. The BCL, we hoped, would benefit from a new opening in democracy, and Adams, who was a Spartan wicket keeper in his time, was in a position of knowledge to take on the challenge. The political leaders in the Barbados Labour Party and the Barbados Congress Party were demanding an end to race and class discrimination, and after the war, when my career took off, they were very vocal in demanding adult suffrage on the basis of one adult one vote.

When I was selected to represent my country in 1945 I was not eligible to vote in a general election. There was no adult suffrage until 1950, and the first election in which I could vote was the following year. The few people who could vote had satisfied the voting authorities that they had a salary which was beyond my imagination, and property with values that classified them as rich. So I was representing my country but my country was not representing me. I could not represent myself in my country in terms of the constitution. This was the peculiar state of affairs in which I tried to craft a career in cricket and at the same time master the craft of batting in order to survive.

Both my captains could vote. Most of the players in the Barbados teams in which I played could vote. So I was a player who was second class politically and economically because I was disenfranchised, and they were not. I would be playing cricket and my team mates would go off to vote in an election and I could not, yet we were in the same team fighting for our country's pride and honour. It was therefore a very simple matter for me to become rather aloof from this situation and take a position on the injustice of it.

By the late 1950s things were changing. The Labour Party governments of the post 1951 period made a substantial impact on these matters, and by 1960 the debates were in full gear. I was courted in the early 60s by both the Barbados Labour Party, and the newly formed Democratic Labour Party that won the general elections in 1961 with Errol Barrow at the helm. I was close to Frank Walcott. He lived in Bank Hall at the time when I made the transition to Empire, and as a fan frequently watched cricket from the club house. He would invite me to cocktail parties where I met gentlemen who wore red ties with a Russian emblem.

I also met Dr. Cummins and Mr. Cox of the Barbados Labour Party, and in the mid-1950s was very supportive of the Federation which was uppermost in their minds and on the political agenda. My experience as a West Indian player with friends across the region made the idea of a Political Federation seemed very logical. I supported it also because we were playing for the West Indies but there was no country called the West Indies. We were a strange concoction. All the other teams we played against were single countries. But we, the West Indians, were playing for a mythical country, a place that did not exist in terms of a constitution.

These were very uplifting times. There was a sense that progress was being made, even though the evidence showed that some of the changes were being compromised by a few politicians who were in politics for business, mostly of a personal kind. But in the villages the poor were getting accustomed to having a voice, to voting, and being listened to in terms of policies and programs. By the time I had finished playing Test cricket in 1958, Barbados was a very different country to the 1948 when I started. By then the BCL had spawned a generation of cricketers, like Gary Sobers who broke the World Record in that year.

On the 1950 tour to England I met the young Errol Barrow. I spent some time with him, along with Forbes Burnham and young Michael Manley. Allan Rae, our opening batsman from Jamaica, knew Manley very well who in turn placed us in contact with West Indian students in England who were to return to the region and participate in changing the political landscape. Allan and I were good friends. We had been to India in 1949, and we were not bad cooks. Errol told me of his intentions to return home and participate in the forging of a more radical brand of labour politics. I remained a little cautious of the party political system.

Frankly, I was slightly afraid of party politics in those days, because you had to deal with some very strange and ugly situations. I knew my roots and wanted to deal with them in a comprehensive fashion, without a sense of divisiveness. I wanted to help my community, but at the same time I was not keen on begging funds from persons in Strathclyde and Belleville. As a youth my kind from the other side of the track in Bridgetown were not allowed into these neighbourhoods. Inhabitants would have unleashed their dogs on seeing the threat. I was not ready to smile with them in order to win a vote.

Later in life I started to open up a bit more. Even then I was very aware that some people looked upon me as a famous cricketer, and not a human being. They want to know nothing else about you. They would invite you to their parties when it suited them for Everton Weekes to be there. I was not very happy with that sort of behaviour, especially from people who had gone on and forgotten their roots. I preferred to stay away, because I was not going to be comfortable. I did not trust myself not to say something I would regret.

But the society was evolving around us, and it was being said that we were witnessing a fundamental transition from the old to the new. I knew a lot of people who decided to leave Barbados, disenchanted for one reason or another with the society. Some professional blacks were not prepared to live through the pain of being second class in their own country. Many packed up because of the slow pace of change.

Mr. Vaz, a prominent industrialist with influence in the cricket arrangements in Jamaica, invited me in 1947 to live and play cricket for the country. I was in the Army, and could not accept the invitation. But I did tell him that Frank would be interested in setting up in Jamaica, and that is how it started. Frank lived there for a year before going off to England where he joined Radcliffe as a professional in the Central Lancashire League. He returned to Jamaica after his retirement and worked for the University of The West Indies at the Mona campus as Director of Sports. He was made a Senator in the government, and played cricket for a team called Boys Town, a working boys club in Kingston where he made a considerable contribution to youth development.

There were other forms of injustices in West Indies cricket that were more disturbing because larger numbers of people were involved. The principal one of these was the exclusion of the Leeward and Windward islands. The players from these island perceived the West Indies Cricket Board of Control (WICBC)in much the same way that we in the BCL saw the BCA. There was no doubt that an injustice was inflicted upon these islands and the people there had every good reason to feel upset about it. It was particularly sad for us in the regional teams because we knew that they had good players, but the officials of the 'big four'- Barbados, British Guiana, Trinidad and Tobago and Jamaica- controlled West Indies cricket administration.

My domestic record shows that I scored five centuries in regional matches, and none against the Leewards and the Windwards. These Islands were not included in the regional competition. I never played competition games against the Windwards, who were our neighbours, though we played against them in friendly games. The good cricketers in the Leewards and Windwards really missed out at the regional and Test levels. They played between themselves, but the West Indies selectors were not falling over themselves to give them opportunities.

It is interesting how an injustice, once it is set in train, can become a norm for a long period. After a while it was easy for players from the 'big four' to assume, and some said it, that there were no good players in these islands. But it was not true. If you say something long enough it can become common-sense until a martyr comes along and takes a stand against it.

For instance, there was a chap named Frank Mason who played for St. Vincent and the Windward Islands. He was a fast bowler, and had apparently bowled down Frank Worrell a couple of times in the friendlies in St. Lucia. Frank pressured the WICBC to invite him to trials between 1954 and 1957, but was not successful. He would have been an excellent prospect against the English in 1954 and the Australians in 1955 when we lacked a genuine pace attack to assist Ram and Val.

It was said that they were not excluded. Rather it was a question of their cricket not being adequately organized. For sure that was a part of the problem, but I would not like to stick my neck out that this was the main reason. I do not think that there was any anxiety on the part of the WICBC to expose these boys to the highest level. I played a lot of friendly games in Antigua when I coached there in 1956. I was under contract to carry out a coaching tour for the Bermudez Biscuit Company based in Trinidad but with a sizeable market in these islands. In 1956 I saw this young cricketer from St. Vincent who played with the Windward Islands. He was already a good looking player, but there was no local support for him, and he went off to university in Montreal. I had arranged with the Biscuit Company to move him to Trinidad and to expose him to regional cricket there, but it did not work out as I had wished.

Tim Hector, the late commentator and writer from Antigua, had an interesting perspective on this matter. He was of the opinion that if an island had no sugar industry, it had no social links to the rulers of West Indies cricket who were the 'sugar boys' of the region. When we speak about the 'big four' the term has to do with the sugar industry because Barbados is not physically a big island in the Eastern Caribbean.

Regional cricket was built around the interests of the sugar planters. If an island had no vibrant sugar plantations, it was unlikely to have developed cricket facilities. Certainly it would have no political lobby to represent the players. When the sugar industry in the Leewards and Windwards was put to the sword, cricket there was put on the back burner where it simmered and never boiled. Barbados had sugar plantations, so too did Trinidad, British Guiana, Jamaica, and to a lesser extent St. Kitts. In the Windward and most of the Leeward islands the sugar planters had ran off, shut down, or were silenced. In the 'big four' the sugar planters and their merchant allies built and funded clubs, and bankrolled competitions. They built club grounds on their lands in town and country to allow their workers to play. By giving the workers time off to play cricket, and by finding jobs for players who they wanted around, they created a system of patronage without which the game would have struggled to survive.

There is an interesting story which is a part of this history. When the Slade Lucas team from England came to the West Indies in 1895, it reported playing in Barbados against an all-white side; the same was true in all the other islands except Antigua where they encountered a team of blacks. The Antiguans could not find any white players to engage the English because the sugar industry had collapsed and with it the white community's financial commitment to the game. It was not until the era of Andy Roberts and Viv Richards, seventy five years later, that the Antiguans got to the centre of things as far as West Indies cricket is concerned.

During this period I developed intimacy with players and conditions in Trinidad. I knew well Parry Jones, Lance Pierre,

Tang Choon, Jeffrey Stollmeyer, and Gerry Gomez. Andy Ganteaume and Kenny Trestrail were sound players who both scored centuries against Barbados in my time. Trinidad was a powerful team, which probably explained why we did best against them. In my first match for Barbados, for example, we were defeated by 10 wickets at Queen's Park Oval, despite Clyde's century in the second innings. We were bundled out for 203 and 265, against the Trinidad total of 427 that included 125 by Trestrial and 132 by Tang Choon.

The following match a week later was drawn. Frank and John Goddard got centuries 113 and 164 not out respectively, but a dogged second innings 108 not out by Gomez saved Trinidad from defeat. The following year we had two drawn games as a result of big scores on both sides. In the January game Ganteaume and Trestrial got centuries, and in the February game Clyde got 314 not out and Frank 255, but with Trestrial getting 151 and Gomez 213 not out there was no advantage to either side. We did not play Trinidad in 1947 or 1948 but when hostilities resumed in January 1949 at Kensington we had the upper hand in the first game, thanks to a first innings total of 698 that included 168 by A.M. Taylor, 149 by R.E. Marshall, and 216 not out by Johnny Lucas. In the February game we returned to the pattern of high scoring drawn games. Three centuries were scored on our side; Marshall 110 run out in the first innings, and in the second innings the in-form Johnny Lucas continued his plunder with 158; C.B. Williams scored a patient 108.

The cricket culture in Trinidad was the most liberal in the region. Like Barbados they had club rivalry, but there all the races played together in the national team in a way that seemed progressive and noble to us. They had the enormous advantage of having in their ranks the great Learie Constantine who was one of the most influential player in West Indies cricket during the 1930s. It was he who wrote and spoke about the need for a political change in West Indies cricket. Barbados was still in denial. It is true that Herman Griffith had argued the Barbados case but he was not a Constantine. Headley, of course was the star player, but it was Learie who had the political influence regionally and internationally. Headley admired him, and considered him the intellectual leader of West Indies cricket.

Trinidad was reinforced with the intellectual ammunition of CLR James who was Constantine's friend and literary collaborator. Constantine began the business of writing cricket books at an early age, and persuaded James to do the same. During the 1930s Constantine, using his enormous influence in the UK, wrote and published a number of important books on West Indies cricket. He was really the first black player to begin the practice of writing books about the game.

His books were not just about the game as played. He was not a cricket journalist. His books were about the politics and sociology of the game. I was too young to know the issues that urged him to write his first famous book, *Cricket and I*, which was published in 1933, but I had heard that he was a no-nonsense, highly political man, and he wanted justice for all within the game. We did not produce a man of that stature in Barbados. Neither did we produce a CLR James who took on board the history of the game as his personal agenda when he began the campaign in 1957 to get Frank appointed captain of the West Indies team.

I met James and had a long chat with him in England 1950. He was not very happy at the time because he was very close to Learie Constantine, and there was some issue that bothered him. He also spoke a great deal about politically organizing the blacks in the USA and how he was deported. I thought at the time I could sit back and listen to him for 24 hours; he was a very gripping speaker. It was clear that he was the kind of man who would fight to get what he considered the right thing. When he took up the captaincy case I was comforted from this point of view because I knew he was clever and very determined.

So I made my Test debut, like Frank and Clyde, in 1948, the same year that the University of the West Indies was established. I was told later that it was also the year in which apartheid was proclaimed the official policy of South Africa. And of course Headley captaining the West Indies Cricket team in the 1948 Test match signaled the end of apartheid in the leadership of West Indies cricket. That I made my debut in the one and only match that Headley captained meant much to me. I cannot think of a more perfect beginning to a Test career in the West Indies.

SIX

LOST IN BARBADOS:
FOUND IN BOMBAY

WHEN I ENTERED THE BCL I HAD NO IDEA that one day I would be walking out on Kensington representing the West Indies in a Test match. Test cricket seemed beyond the imagination, almost cosmic in terms of earth time. I had no reason to think otherwise at age 13. There was little around me to suggest that this path lay ahead. The stories that circulated in the gap were not encouraging.

Uppermost in my mind at that time were the sad tales about the number of youngsters before me who were rated as excellent in the village but who ended up drinking their lives away or ran into difficulty with the law. There were endless reports of young boys who stopped playing suddenly and vowed never to touch a cricket ball again. These were tragic accounts that had an impact on my mind.

But I loved batting, and wanted to master the art. It did not matter if I were in a dead end situation. I imagined being boxed in with nowhere to go, and I feared the possibility of disillusionment. I saw young men exit their teens and disappeared from the cricket scene; another generation entered and the cycle started all over again. My cousin who took me to Westshire tried to shield me from this world of fear and doubt. He urged and showed me how to keep the faith.

The important thing for me was to understand why this was the case; why so many youngsters from the villages with the skills never moved out of the BCL into the national team. I also needed to be sure that these youngsters were as good as people had said. Slowly I began to piece together the facts which were later confirmed when I entered the Barbados team. I learned to have confidence in my ability to research and interpret situations in which I found myself. It helped my cricket at the crease; batting, after all, is built on skill, confidence, and resolve.

With all the mental and physical preparation that is possible there is no way of knowing how you will respond to the atmosphere of your first Test match. In my case it was like something from a science fiction film. I could have been abducted by aliens and taken to another planet. I remember as clearly now as I did then. Here is it, a confession so to speak. It was my turn to bat. I stepped onto the field. On the way to the middle my mind went into a kind of trance and I didn't know where I was. I had walked out to bat at Kensington several times before but on this occasion something weird occurred. The grass didn't feel the same; it was not the Kensington outfield I knew. I thought I was stepping higher than normal, as if walking barefooted on a hot road. It was an attack of nervousness; I so badly wanted to do well.

It was a strange beginning. In the first innings we were all out for 296. Stollmeyer led with 78, and Gomez top scored with 86. I chipped in with 35 followed by Headley with 29. Jim Laker had an excellent spell of spin, picking up 7 for 103 from 37 overs. The important thing about this spell was that he bowled down four of his victims including Clyde, Gomez and Headley. In the second innings my disappointment with scoring 25 was set aside by the disbelief in seeing Robert Christiani, also in his first Test match, given out lbw on 99. Laker did not bowl me down in the first innings, but in the second innings, in which Howorth picked up 6 for 124 from 41 overs, I was the only person he cleaned bowled.

Kensington looked a very different place. My boots were not touching the grass. I have never discussed this experience with anyone, but I know that other players have had similar experiences. I understood later that I was in fact a nervous starter. I walked to the wicket with a heightened feeling of nervousness which would last for the first over. This condition persisted during my entire career. It was especially intense for the first couple of balls. I would say to myself before facing each ball: 'this delivery is not going to get me out....this delivery is not going to get me out.' That determination was there at all times. It was the first and foremost of my thoughts. Even though I was rated a stroke player I would admit that I was not the best starter in the world. But after a couple of balls a feeling of calm would emerge and I would be fine.

In this first Test pitch conditions were not the best for batting. We were playing on a wet surface, and it was two paced, which was unusual for Kensington. We had a lot of rain during the week, which is why the spinners on both sides did so well. In England's second innings Goddard picked up two wickets bowling his off spin. I did not focus attention on whether it was better for me to debut in Barbados or overseas. Over time I developed a preference for playing outside of Barbados, because at home so much is expected of you. This feeling became even stronger after we returned from India in 1949, which was my second series for the West Indies and where I had done quite well.

I scored my first Test century during the last game at Sabina Park. Batting at no. 3, and surrounded by a world of troubles, I scored 141 in a match that we won by 10 wickets. The next highest score in the innings was 75 by W. Ferguson batting at no. 9. Hinds Johnson, our pacer picked up five wickets in each innings, enabling us to win the series 2-0. I had followed my 35 and 25 in the first Test with 36 and 20 in the second Test at Queen's Park Oval which was also drawn. In the third Test at Bourda I was dropped down from no.3 to no. 7, and Clyde was promoted to the no. 3 spot. We won the game by 7 wickets largely due to a brilliant 131 by Frank and a five wicket haul by Goddard, our skipper.

At Sabina Park for the fourth Test I was returned to no. 3 and things began to click into place. It was the first time I had gotten over the early start blues and built an inning in the way I was accustomed. My first Test century came after five innings. Subsequently, there was a general view that I was out of the blocks. Frank led the way among the 3Ws with the first Test century, but Clyde was tied up in wicket keeper duties and was not as fresh when batting as he would have liked.

After Sabina Park we were off to India where I found fuel and took flight. The first Test was played at Delhi. It was a drawn game, but for us it was also a run fest. We put them to the sword early scoring 631 in the first innings. Clyde, still the wicket keeper, was now among the big runs, hitting the top score of 152. He never looked like getting out, and as fate would have it he was run out. Gomez followed with 101, and coming in at no. 7 somehow I was able to scramble to 128, and R.J Christiani batting at no. 8, finished with 107.

Frank was not with us on this tour. There were some personal issues with the WICBC that could have been resolved in a fashion that would have allowed him to tour. Frank tried to accommodate the Board but it was not prepared to show any flexibility. He was the first professional player amongst us in the Test team at the time. He played in the English league in order to make a living which Test cricket could not provide in an honourable way. Most of the white players in the team were persons with professions, or had land and property that earned then a secure living. Frank had no sponsor and he asked the WICBC for a tour salary of 300 pounds. The WICBC refused. Frank indicated that he would tour on the offered conditions, and would continue the salary discussion at a later date. This was not accepted. We missed him very much.

I had now scored two centuries in succession. For the second Test I was moved up to no. 4, behind Clyde at three. Again, we notched up a formidable total of 629, with Allan Rae leading the way with an elegant 104. Clyde was run out again, this time on 68 and I went on to score 194. We bowled out the Indians for 273, enforced the follow on, but there was no time to press for victory. In the third Test at Calcutta, which was also drawn, I scored 162 in the first innings and 101 in the second. Clyde made 108. In the fourth Test it was my turn to get run out, which I did on 90 in a game which we won by an innings and 193 runs. There were no West Indies centuries in the fifth Test at Bombay which was drawn, leaving us with a 1-0 series victory.

I returned from India feeling that I had mastered the Test game and that I would be fine for the future. I had scored five consecutive Test centuries establishing, a new world record, which I thought was not bad for a little chap on his second tour. It was the final layer on the cake, the first of which was baked in the BCL oven, and the second in the cauldron of the BCA. It all seemed like a steep curve, an Everest in fact from the point of view of the New Orleans kid. First, I could not have imagined getting the opportunity, and here I was scoring runs in far away places as if I was on a field somewhere in Bridgetown.

There was a clear connection between the skills I had honed in the BCL and the discipline required to score heavily in India where the pitches were not like any we had at home. They were drier, slower, dustier, and had less bounce. But they required a great deal of care, especially against the seasoned spinners India turned out. Also, it seemed that I had settled into being a regular no. 4 batsman, a position I had no problems with. The nervousness was still there, but I was learning how to manage it more skillfully.

There were some experiences on this tour that have remained with me. In some respects you never forget the first lessons because they are instrumental in determining the outcomes of later events. I had made a decision that I would never hit the first ball for four, even if it was a long hop or a full pitch. Second, I never played from the shoulders until I was 15 or 20 minutes into my innings. I would use my wrist and lower arm to push the ball around. Sometimes pushing would bring you a four if the timing is good, and you are able to beat the field. In those days there was no sweeper patrolling the cover boundary. Third, I tried to understand the thinking of my captain and to be a part of the strategy being worked out. It is very difficult to play top class cricket if you are at odds with your captain. You need the peace of mind to focus on the job at hand.

I was very fortunate to play my first Test under the aura of 'Mas George'. It was like a dream that came true because he was my idol. I felt he wanted me to do well in my first outing. Frank did not play in that game. He had food-poisoning or some other stomach ailment. But George was a shrewd captain. He handled the match with great skill. In the evenings we had long chats and I could feel the knowledge coming from between his ears. He spoke a lot about our disastrous tour to Australia in 1931. It was like sitting back in school and listening to a favourite teacher. He was wounded by the defeat 'down under', despite his outstanding personal performance.

During the Test, George developed problems with his lower back, and did not play for the remainder of the series. He was slated to captain the first and the fourth Tests. These decisions were made in advance. The WICBC allocated the captain for two matches and we had three standing captains. This was part of the confusion with George. He was the best batsman, certainly in the Caribbean, and most probably in the world. But there was something that was not right and I would not like to think it was his colour or his position in life.

The match itself was a challenge to my personal faith in the values of cricket I had acquired in the BCL and in the gaps of New Orleans. I was very disappointed with the 35 runs I scored in the first innings because I was batting well I thought. A ball from Tremlett gave my gloves the finest possible brush on the way to keeper Godfrey Evans who caught it and did not appeal. He threw it back to the bowler who did not raise an eyebrow.

Two balls later a similar thing happened and this time I walked. An attack of guilt I presumed. I had the opportunity to go on because nobody appealed. I became very friendly with Evans, and the two captains on tour, K. Cranston and Gubby Allen. We would make jokes about these things, but they were the kind of gentlemen who would have appealed only if they thought I had gotten a touch.

If Kensington was personally interesting, the Sabina Park match was publicly controversial and embarrassing. George was expected to play but persistent back problems ruled him out. The Jamaican crowd favoured its home boy, J.K. Holt as his replacement. Headley, I was told, had expressed a preference for me in his place. The plane to Jamaica arrived late. Flying over Kingston we saw that the game had already started. I did not know if I was listed in the final team. I got to the hotel and the first question I asked an official was "is Weekes in the team?" I was told yes, and that J. K. Holt was substituting for me on the field. I rushed to the ground and walked on to the field amidst loud boos and what seemed like a lifetime of jeering. It was not a very pleasant entrance. I was taken by surprise because the previous year I was so well received when I had scored 97 and 123 in two regional matches.

Well, it was one of those biblical moments. One minute the crowd was shouting 'hang him' and the next they were calling 'hail the Massiah cometh' because I went on to make my first Test century, 141 in the first innings from a winning total of 490. Furthermore, it was a deepening of my ongoing love affair with Jamaica. Not only did I enjoy being in Jamaica, where I had made some very good friends, but I felt comfortable on the pitches there and scoring runs seemed less challenging than some other places. The crowd was not personal in its jeering. It was part of a long tradition in which countries would favour the local lad if the other choices were not performing at the approved level.

My low scores to date were not exactly the stuff that endeared me to the crowd in the face of a youngster who had sound credentials. Scores of 35, 25, 36, 20 and 36 were not disastrous but they signaled that I lacked what it took to go on after good starts. This was as disturbing to me as it was irritating to the crowds and the selectors. These low scores were made against the background of hundreds by G.M. Carew(107) and A.G. Ganteaume(112) in the second Test and Frank (131 not out) in the third; not to mention the 78, 86, and 99 in the first Test by Stollmeyer, Gomez and Christiani respectively, and the 97 and 62 in the second Test by Frank and Gomez respectively.

But it was not that J.K. had a superior record that was impatient of debate. He had been a little patchy in the regional competition, but what made his case was an excellent 172 he scored against British Guiana in October the previous year. The Jamaican crowd was keen to see J.K. make his Test debut, and they were quite correct in this because they knew him as an impressive batsman. This had been a feature of West Indies cricket. It is not that local fans are unfair in their preference for a local boy. It is that they would have seen more of their local lad than the chap who gets the selectors' nod.

J.K. did eventually make his test debut, but it was six years later in the 1954 England tour of the West Indies. He also made it in the first Test at Sabina Park in front of his home crowd that had long felt an injustice was done to him. He batted at no. 3 and scored an impressive 94 in the first innings that helped to set up a West Indies victory by 140 runs. It was the highest score for any West Indies batsman in that Test. Frank did not play in that game and Clyde and I scored 65 and 55 respectively. We made a total of 417, after which, thanks to the spin twins, Ram and Val, we wrapped up England for 170. We pushed on the advantage and skipper Stollmeyer declared on 209 for 6 after I had posted 90 not out on the board.

Interpersonal politics were rampant in West Indies cricket, and it came as a surprise to many people, though not to me, that Stollmeyer should have declared on my innings at 90 in a game that had plenty of time. Also, in a first Test when we wanted to impress our superiority upon the visitors. It appeared that I was on my way to another century at Sabina Park. My last occasion was against India the previous year in which I scored 109 in the second innings along with Frank and Clyde who had made 237 and 118 respectively.

Needless to say it was a declaration that sent tongues wagging and questions being asked about the intentions of Stollmeyer. I did not participate in the speculation, though I was asked pointed questions by many people as to the nature of our relationship. Suffice it to say that I saw no compelling cricketing reason for the skipper's decision at the moment, and it did create a state of affairs we did not need. On reflection one could see some of the human elements creeping into the decision making process that required a bigness of mind which is very rare in most circumstances.

In the 1948 tour we, the 3Ws, made our Test debut. In the first Test Frank did not play and in the second Test at Queen's Park Oval we played together for the first time. The order was Weekes(3), Worrell(4) and Walcott(5). In the first innings we scored 36, 97, and 20 respectively. Clyde was the keeper, and Frank bowled 37 overs of seamers in the game, and picked up one wicket, opener S.C Griffith, trapped lbw. We played again in the third Test at Bourda, where Frank had scored the brilliant match winning 131 not out in the first innings. The Sabina Park Test in which I scored the 141 Frank had made 38 and Clyde 45.

When we went off to India without Frank at the end of the year, where I scored the four consecutive centuries, Clyde made 152 in the first Test, 68 in the second, 54 and 108 in the third, and 43 in the fourth. Then we had the glory tour of England in 1950 that brought great credit to captain Goddard, some of which he lost against Australia the following year. By the time we got home to meet the English in 1954, Stollmeyer was captain and certain attitudes were well in train about the 3Ws.

There were many stories about the J.K. incident at Sabina. When I arrived on the field and J.K. ran off, the crowd erupted into jeering. Shortly thereafter Evans drove a ball from Kentish our pacer to cover and I took the catch. When I saw the ball coming for a moment I imagined dropping it and being dragged off the field by an angry crowd to a nearby gallows. My life flashed before my eyes and to this day I cannot recall whether objectively it was a difficult or simple catch. It seemed enormously difficult, in fact near impossible. The jeering abated a little but not by much so deep was the rage about J.K.'s non-selection.

We bowled out England for 227, thanks to a spell of fine pace bowling by Hinds Johnson who took 5 for 41, and Clyde's four dismissals behind the stumps. The next day, two wickets went down fairly cheaply, Goddard for 17 and Stollmeyer for 30, both going to Howorth, the spinner. As I came out the dressing room and entered the field, the booing started once again, this time louder than when I had arrived on the field on the first day. It was hard to imagine at that moment that I was

97

playing for the West Indies, at home, and that I had scored some good runs before this crowd that knew something about me.

It took 25 minutes to get off the mark. Howorth was pitching in the foot marks left behind by Hinds Johnson. The ball was bouncing and turning square, entirely unpredictable. When I went in Frank was at the other end. He looked a little surprised that I was having a rough time. He though maybe it was the booing that had me unsettled, as some of the language was not very complimentary to my dear mother and cannot be repeated here, or anywhere in fact where there is polite society. Then, after about 20 minutes, I under-edged one from Howorth that went through the keeper's gloves and struck him on the pads. Normally, Geoffrey Evans would throw up these simple catches, but the Lord saved me that day, for the second time.

Had I scored 0 before this crowd, blood would have been spilt that day. Talking through things with Frank in the middle, I eventually settled down, and started to score freely. When I eventually got out, caught by Len Hutton off J.T. Ikin, the same crowd ran onto the field and lifted me off in triumph. I must confess that when I saw the crowd approaching my knees got a little weak, and maybe the bladder was to follow. But I saw a few smiles, and before I knew it, I was hoisted into the air. This is a West Indian thing. I don't think it happens anywhere else. It is the story of my first Test hundred.

But the tale began much earlier. I was lucky to have reached Jamaica because Jack Kidney, the WICB official, was travelling there for a Board meeting. I had no confirmed seat and he gave me his. He actually got off the plane to allow me to travel. The plane went first to Venezuela, and then to Santo Domingo where it was delayed for three or four hours. By this time I was a bag of nerves. There had been no specific communication from the WICB; I was told to catch the plane and join the squad in Kingston. I didn't know if I was in the final XI.

When I was taken off the field, 'Mas George' came over and seemed very happy about the performance. He would call me 'young man', and he said 'not bad young man; your first hundred, I am happy for you'. That was what he said to me. It was very comforting coming from him. He was walking away, stopped, and turned and said, 'you are going to make many more'.

In India I roomed with George. He played in the first Test at Delhi, scored two, and his back problems flared up. He did not play again during the series. He was not very mobile because of this. To add insult to his pain, he would wake me up to say that he could not sleep because I was snoring too loudly. Then he would go off to sleep, snore like one of those old diesel engines, and I would be up all night because I dare not wake up this legend, this 'elephant' in the room, as the Americans would say.

Finally, I struck up the courage to ask the manager to relieve me of this pressure. Of course I could not, as a youngster, make negative comments on my room mate. So what I did was to indicate that in the opinion of the team a player of George's standing should have a single room and not be inconvenienced by the coming and going of a young player. It was agreed. The big man got his single room and Clyde and I hooked up and stayed that way for a long time.

Sabina Park, then, was a life changing experience. It was an emotional and physical experience that resembled an initiation into a secret military society. For sure it was a baptism of fire, and with the grace of the Almighty all I had learned before came to the fore, and to the rescue. As in all things a little luck goes a long way. I was determined to help myself by developing my mind game to the maximum.

I do not know how or why it came to me as a teenager that the mind game was 75% of success. But I knew that one had to be smart in order to be in the game, and that there were some very fine players out there competing for the few spaces in the West Indies team. I saw the Sabina Park experience as an extension of the mind game I had been practicing as a teenager; how to stay focus and to concentrate as I faced every ball as if it was coming to take my life away. That is how I felt; each ball had the potential to take my life, and livelihood away, and I was fighting with all my might.

After Sabina Park I felt comfortable that I was getting on top of the plan. The century was fine, but it was played against considerable adversity and under very unfavourable circumstances. It helped to know that George was rooting for me, but I could hear the boys from the BCL years saying, 'come on Evee, stick in and grind them to dust'. They helped me to get through the 25 minutes it took to get off the mark. Importantly, my BCL exposure, the rough ragging I got from crowds as a youth, helped me to understand that it was not personal; it was cricket business and the hostility could be washed away by a good innings. It was all about winning hearts and minds, and only good cricket can win West Indian hearts and minds.

I was batting with all of this in mind as I played each ball. I knew that the game was bigger than each player, and if I respected the game it would give me respect. At the end of it I though that maybe I was good for at least another game. In those days scoring a century was no proof that you would be selected. The politics of selection could see you sitting out the next game as someone else came back to take his place. So there were no certainties. I went back to my own experience. I had to over-perform in order to get the selectors' nod. In other words, I had to make it difficult, embarrassing for them to leave me out. George would have lobbied for me but he was not a selector. And even with this hundred I still felt vulnerable.

Press reports were encouraging. A lead writer thought that I had some ability, and suggested that I should be selected for the tour to India. I had my own deep reservations. But I resolved that if that door was opened it would be hell to get me out of that room. I braced myself for the news, and when it came I went off to India with my mind made up.

Between the Sabina Park match and the tour to India later in the year, I took up a contract to play for Bacup in the Lancashire League. It was an opportunity to do as Frank had done, earn some income and learn the English conditions. I had heard a great deal about the ball moving around in England, and the green tops on which it seamed. The stories about these conditions were many, as were those about the methods and techniques needed to survive. As I was raised to deploy the 'back and across technique' to pace, and to use my feet to spinners, I figured I should catch on pretty quickly. After all, I consider myself a student of the technical and scientific aspects of batting. It was all a central part of what I called the mind game.

When I arrived in India there was nothing like the English conditions I was learning to master. But my keeness to keep an eye on the ball and play it onto the bat was sharpened. India had a bowler named Phadkar who bowled at will some pretty big in-swingers and out-swingers. The English experience in the summer was a great asset in coping with him.

The income from the English summer also helped to take the pressure off the mind. Cricket was my only source of finance. Playing for the West Indies I was an amateur, which meant that I was given a fee to cover out of pocket expenses. I was paid the handsome sum of a pound a day, or something like that. This is what the WICBC gave us when we turned up for Test duty. We went on tour for two or three months at a time on this stipend. But I loved cricket and I played. At the same time I could not meet any financial obligations back home with this stipend, and lived in a constant state of resource embarrassment. This, of course, was not the case with Stollmeyer, Gomez, Goddard, and the others. They were men of means. Frank and I especially felt the financial pinch. As a result he, then I, became professionals playing under contract in the English League.

By this time most English Test players were also professionals. English cricket had been racked by a debate between the wars on whether cricketers should be allowed to turn professionals. The aristocrats and gentry did not favor the professional status, but increasingly more players were coming from the working class, and by my time the argument was won in favour of professionalism. English players were offered contracts with attractive remuneration, and they got a benefit game after ten years.

In the West Indies we remained mostly amateurs. We got eight shirts and six trousers, a blazer, a dress suit and an evening dress suit (grey) for cocktail parties. These were issued to us by the WICBC. When we attended a cocktail party we were expected to look presentable in our blazer. If we had a dinner engagement we wore the lounge suit. I was provided with these items. Beyond that I was on my own.

On tour in India I received a stipend of a pound a day, and tried to save every penny. The feeling at the time in the Caribbean was that the Board should have paid Frank what he asked for. It was not exorbitant; just 300 Pounds. In 1953 when the Indians toured the West Indies Frank was given a contract. By then Clyde, Ram and Val had joined the list. I had been a professional since 1949, but I didn't get a contract. I was paid 15 dollars a day for each Test match; 75 dollars a match.

Frank was a more established player than Clyde and I. He had scored a Test century before the two of us. At the time he was easily the best player in the Caribbean, in my view and we thought he should have been paid to go to India. But the WICB felt that it was a bad precedent. They did not want to open that door. They didn't think he was deserving of it. They figured that we were not ready for that kind of step. The attitude to Frank on the WICBC was 'who does he think he is?' It seemed that way to me. Later on this was confirmed to me. They thought he was 'too previous'.

Frank prepared himself to meet the various charges against him. He was a great man, and many people came to realize this, and expected much of him, especially some of those very people who tried to make his life very difficult. When he became captain of the West Indies team it was final proof of the statement that you cannot keep a good man down. It was a proud and fulfilling moment for Clyde and I because we knew all along that he was the right man for the job, and that he had been ready for a long time before the WICBC agreed to act.

The focus on his university studies helped him to weather the storm. At first he wanted to study something in the field of optics, because he had an interest in eyes. He dropped that and didn't study for some time. Then he turned to Sociology and Economics and completed his degree at Manchester University. I believe he was motivated to acquire academic knowledge because he wanted to work after cricket in helping under-privileged West Indian people.

While in India I felt that Frank would have been excellent. He was a very good player of spin and he was in good form at the end of 1948. While I was racking up the centuries images of Frank batting at the other end would flash through my mind. It was my first encounter with what we now call the Indian spin culture, and I was determined to learn quickly and get to the bottom of whatever mystery there was. I thought that I was a good player of spin before, with an ability to detect early where the ball was going. By concentrating and watching the ball I could see if it was going to spin from leg to off or if it was going to spin from off to leg. I could see from the seam where it was intended to go.

In India the spin was coming from both ends and I had to be able to read it out of the bowler's hand. I felt that if I could pick it up at 22 metres I would be in a better position to play the stroke than if I was picking it up at 10 metres. I needed the extra time to read the ball, remember field placements, and find the boundary. Good readers of spin very seldom get out stumped. You may miss hit, get a little cocky looking to hit over mid-off, and get an outside edge and it goes into the covers and you look very silly, but very seldom you would miss the ball completely. In India I felt very nimble on my feet. I was not the only one. Many of our front line batsmen got runs–Rae, Stollmeyer, Christiani, and Clyde. But I was in a groove and all the parts were moving together–eyes, wrist, feet and shoulders. I was a touch player and needed to feel the inter-connection of these parts. Once they came together, and I felt like a finely tuned engine, I became confident. I worked very hard at creating this condition of mind and body. In India it was reported to me that once I came in to bat and Armarnath, the skipper, said 'give him his hundred and let him go back in.'

I didn't play much in any of the first class matches of the tour because the distances were great, and traveling by train was exhausting. We were traveling long distances, sometimes 9 and 10 hours on a train. After the first Test in Delhi we traveled 14 hours by train to the next venue. In those days Indian trains were not the best in the world. When we came off that train some of the chaps had grown near a half inch of beard. There were tens of thousands of people coming out to see the West Indies. It was the first time they were seeing us. It was our first Test tour to India.

The Indian public certainly got a treat because lots of runs were scored on the tour on both sides. Some pundits have said that it was a tour of great batsmen and average bowlers on both sides. I am not sure about that. Someone came up to me and said that I had broken Headley's record by scoring five centuries in my first nine Tests. I was not aware of these issues. One night listening to Ian Chapell commenting on players of the past 50 years I heard him mention that at one stage my Test average was 87. I did not know this. I was too busy thinking, not counting.

SEVEN

1950 IN ENGLAND:
THE END OF EMPIRE

PLAYING IN THE LANCASHIRE LEAGUE in the summer of 1948 and 1949 helped enormously in my adjustment to Test conditions in England. Bacup, my team, was not just a cricket side; it was a community that fostered a sense of duty and responsibility among players. This was the kind of fine tuning I needed in order to sharpen my focus on the meaning of being a West Indian Test player.

We arrived in England late in the spring of 1950. I was fairly well prepared for the English conditions. I knew the first Test was scheduled for June; this meant chilly days and cold nights. Frank had played in the summer of 1948, and had some experience of the pitches and had seen some of the players first hand. We were the only players with this background, and the team expected us to take the lead in discussion about playing conditions. Ram and Val had played no Test cricket at all.

It was a good summer, cold in June but quite warn in July.

In the early matches I remember praying once or twice that the ball would not come my way. My fingers were numb and at times I could not feel my toes. We were particularly concerned about the impact of the weather on the fingers of Ram and Val, our special weapons. But as it turned out there was no need because they spun us to victory in nearly every game. In the county matches, before the first Test, Val bowled well. I didn't think many of the English batsmen were able to read him although he bowled mostly orthodox spin.

The few good players were able to get some runs. Washbrook got two centuries, Evans one, and Hutton got a double not out at the Oval from a total of 344. Ram's power lay in his accuracy, and he kept batsmen subdued on the best of pitches. With Val, he was able to beat batsmen with good defenses by getting through bat and pad. For the off-break that was pitched wide outside off stump, they didn't pad up in 1950; that came in 1957. They would look to play a stroke, mostly getting back to cut against the spin. Then to the leg break they would push forward and first slip did the rest.

I made a fair amount of runs in the County games. There was one game that stands out in my mind. It was against Cambridge University. They got something like 500 runs against us. It was a three-day game. We ended up with 700 odd. Ram and Val did not play. Ram was more the danger man because he bowled off breaks and leg breaks that turned and bounced. Val was more orthodox. But he spun the ball more than any of the other arm spinners I had seen. You could hear it buzzing when he let it go. And of course he was completely bruised up between the fore finger and the middle finger; you would see the flesh exposed after a few matches.

Val also had a quick, straight one which was like a fast top

107

spinner. Instead of turning away from the right-handed batsman, it would come on to him, and sometimes in straightening it would bounce. As the tour went on, they both got better. There is nothing like getting wickets to build confidence, and they took a lot of wickets.

We didn't do too well in the first Test match. England won by 202 runs. It was played at Old Trafford in early June. Yardley took first knock and his boys piled up 312. It was in this match that Evans, the keeper, got a century (104) and Trevor Bailey was not out on 82. Hinds Johnson, our opening bowler, was the oldest man on the side, 40 or just over, but still very quick. He didn't get any wickets, and neither did Gomez our medium fast seamer. Val did the stuff from the beginning, picking up 8 for 104 from 50 overs. It was quite a majestic performance in a losing game.

We went in and were bundled out for 215; my opening effort of 52 was the highest score. We had an opportunity to get back into the game when we reduced England to 288, but failed miserably in the second innings, bowled out for a mere 183. Stollmeyer scored a patient 78, and everyone else went back to the pavilion with little to talk about. The defeat came as a bit of a shock because we were confident, having defeated England in the Caribbean in 1948. We had never beaten them in England before. But having had the taste of victory in the West Indies we were smelling success.

I had made a pretty sober calculation of our chances. I didn't think we would be able to run through their batting, but I was fairly certain our batting would look after itself. Some people said it was probably the strongest batting side the West Indies had ever had. With Frank, Clyde and myself in the middle, following openers Rae and Stollmeyer, and with Gomez and

Goddard in the lower half, I thought such an assessment seemed reasonable.

I was impressed with the young and very capable Roy Marshall, who didn't play in any of the Test matches. In my humble opinion he was a very good player. We used the same openers throughout the tour, and this was bad news for Roy. I had seen neither Ram nor Val before and had no idea what we had bought into. It was an extraordinary situation to rely during an overseas tour, on a spin attack that had to learn everything on the job. If any selector did that today he would be fired immediately. We went to England to play a series without any significant preparation whatsoever, and with players who met each other for the first time at a train station.

This was our first tour after the War. Ram and Val had both played a few matches in the regional competition, and had played against each other at Queens Park Oval earlier in the year. So at least they knew each other and had some basis on which to see themselves as a partnership. In the first of those two matches, Trinidad vs. Jamaica, Ram picked up 8 wickets and Val none. In the second game Val picked up two and Ram four. In the first game in which Val took no wicket he had bowled 39 overs at a cost of 111 runs. Trinidad had scored a massive 581 for 2 declared because openers Ganteaume and Stollmeyer had made 147 and 261 respectively, followed by 161 from Trestrail. So there was not much, on paper, to recommend the gentlemen.

Our opening bowler was Hinds Johnson, 40 years, but still our fastest. Prior Jones was a fine pace bowler but I did not expect him to tear through a team, neither did I expect it of Lance Pierre. There were a useful pace attack for Trinidad but against England I had my doubts. Prior Jones was the best of the three but not by much. He was not as fast as Hinds Johnson, but he moved the ball through the air and off the pitch. So the bowling attack wasn't first rate, but was respectable.

As it turned out the pacers had less work to do than anticipated. From the first Test, as soon as the pacers bowled a few overs and the shine was off, Ram and Val were called into the attack. In the first Test, for example, Val bowled 50 and 56 overs in the first and second innings respectively, while Ram bowled 39 and 42. Johnson on the other hand bowled 10 in the first and did not bowl in the second. Neither Jones nor Pierre was selected for the first Test, and we relied on Goddard and Gomez, and to a lesser extent Frank to do the seam bowling.

I discovered, however, that only two English batsmen were able to read Ram. Those two, funnily enough were Hutton, the opener, and Evans the keeper. The others were more than a little uncomfortable. Hutton was a class player, no doubt about it; and a very sensible player at that. At times he would give the other opener most of the strike, especially if the bowler was generating pace off the wicket with bounce. It looked that way to me. You have to be very clever to do things like this. It is the reaction of a thinking player.

In the first Test Val picked up Hutton in the first innings, and Frank did the honours in the second. When we got to Lords for the second Test, Val picked him up in both innings fairly cheaply. It was a dog fight, the second Test. I knew we had to capitalize on our strength and attack the English bowling, and throw Ram and Val at them from the first ball. I was not too disheartened by the defeat. I had seen the weaknesses of the English team during the process. Rae gave us a good start with his 106, and Frank and I were able to chip in with half centuries; 52 and 63 respectively. We reached a total of 326 runs, which was respectable at Lords, and then we brought out the dogs of war and unleashed them on England.

It was like clockwork. Jones was brought into the side instead of Johnson, and Goddard gave him a few overs. He bowled well but did not pick up any wickets in his first spell. In all he bowled 8 overs and picked up 1 for 13. Frank bowled a few, as did Goddard and Gomez. But it was Ram and Val that did the damage. Ram picked up 5 for 66 from 43 overs, and Val 4 for 48 from 45 overs. England was all out for 151. It was an enormous effort, and it spun us back into the series with a win by 326 runs. In the second innings Clyde unleashed his power on the attack and his 168 not out was as dominant an innings as it is possible to imagine.

Clyde innings has often overshadowed his very effective wicket keeping in the match. But in England first innings he was responsible for four dismissals, including the stumping of both openers, Hutton and Washbrook off Val and Ram respectively. I scored 63 for the second time in the match but it was a joy to watch Clyde plundering the bowling. We declared for 425 in our second innings and dismissed England in the second innings for 274. The same formula was used by Goddard. Jones, Worrell, Gomez and Goddard put in short spell, and the bulk of the bowling was done by the spin twins. Val bowled 71 overs and picked up 3 for 79 while Ram bowled 72 overs and finished with 6 for 86.

What I remember most about my knock of 63 in the first innings was that I had to use every skill I could muster, concentration and technique, in order to handle the swing of Alec Bedser. In the end I got an inside edge, on to the pad, and the ball found its way into the stumps. Bedser was the master of seam bowling. He was the classical English seamer, not quick, but he moved the ball through the air and off the wicket. At Lords he was bowling with great skill and bowled down Frank, Christaini and myself in the first innings. There was a little grass on the pitch and he made the ball wobble in the most amazing way. We did very well to master him, a tribute I suppose to the skill of our batsmen, especially Rae who faced the new ball and scored an excellent 106. In the end Bedser bowled 40 overs and conceded just 60 runs while picking up 3 wickets.

In the second innings, Bedser was at it again. He really was the consummate swing bowler. He got just one wicket, but bowled 44 overs, 16 maidens, and conceded just 80 runs. I looked into the heavens for help because with a little grass on the pitch, and cloud cover, Bedser would have been more than a handful. It was a personal challenge facing him. I did not fear him because I felt quite good about my technique.

Clyde used his height and reach with maximum effect. He would reach out, and getting to the pitch, drive Bedser's outswinger. Then he used his left foot to play the inswinger as it dipped. It was always a greater challenge facing swing bowlers like Bedser and Bailey because they did much more with the ball than the quick men. I saw inexperience batsmen going for the big cover drive to what looked like a half volley, just to see their middle or leg stump out the ground as the ball would swing late.

I knew how to reach out to the in-ducker, left elbow out, low backlift and to punch it into the covers, or caress it through extra cover with a straight bat. In many respects I was blessed with having learnt the art and science of batting the way I did, in the villages and in the clubs. I can think of no other reason why I succeeded against such excellent bowling.

When we moved to Trent Bridge for the third Test the

thinking in the camp was that England was feeling the pressure of our high performance. Moving north from London is always risky in June and July because the weather could change suddenly, and not for the better. But Trent Bridge has always been a good place for batsmen, and I was confident I would get some runs. Of course neither Frank nor I had made a century so far, and I had the bit in my mouth. Clyde had licked the leather off the ball at Lords, and it was only reasonable that the two of us should follow. Since the media were dubbing us the 3Ws, and we were getting used to the term, we wanted to live up to the expectation that anything one did so would the others.

England took first knock and was bundled out for 223. Johnson came back into the side to replace Jones and bowled very well, fast and hostile, and picked up 3 for 59 from 25 overs. Ram and Val got two wickets each from lengthy spells. It was Frank who picked up three in a spell of 17 overs, conceding just 40 runs. It was he and Johnson who ripped through the top order, exposing the bottom half to Ram and Val. Skipper Yardley batted well for a dogged 41. Hutton did not play in this game, and this weakened the team considerably. England was lucky to reach 223, as they were 75 for 5; the tail wagged, and two bowlers, Shackleton (42) and Jenkins(39), batting at nos. 8 and 9 respectively, held up our assault.

Rae and Stollmeyer, once again, gave us a good start. The first wicket fell at 77. It was here that Frank and I took the opportunity to join with Clyde and gave the West Indies the commanding position we were looking for in response to England. Bedser was up to his usual trick, and picked up 5 for 127 from a long spell of 48 overs, but we were ready for him. Frank was magnificent. His innings of 261 has been hailed as a classic in stroke play. I can verify this because I was at the other end. My own 129 was in support of Frank, and it was a real pleasure batting with him, once again. The bowlers had no answer to his shots because his footwork was perfect and his balance outstanding.

I got to my 100 late in the evening with two fours off Bedser through the covers – widish balls. When I got back to the crease the following morning, I thought that it was a good thing I had reached the century before because I was scrambling to touch the swinging ball. He got rid of Frank pretty early, but I was determined that he would not get me. I watched him like a hawk, not scoring but sticking it out. Then a chap called Eric Hollies took me out, caught and bowled for 129. The tail collapsed after that; our last 6 wickets fell for less than 50 runs because Bedser bowled Clyde for 8, and wrapped up the rest. We had posted 558 and England was in a very deep hole.

I expected the English to fight back, and they did. They went off to a flying start, posting 212 for the first wicket thanks to another century by Washbrook(102) and 94 by R.T Simpson who had replaced Hutton. But Ram and Val soon got going, and though the top order posted an additional three 50s, Ram ended with 5 for 135 from 81 overs, an extraordinary bowling feat for a man in his first Test series. Words cannot describe the value this man brought to West Indies cricket, and with no background to speak of at all in terms of having a distinguished regional record. Val chipped in with 3 for 140 from 92 overs, suggesting that batsmen could not get him off the square. We were left with just under a 100 to win and these were knocked off by Stollmeyer (52) and Rae (46) without any fuss. It was a convincing victory by 10 wickets that placed us in the drivers' seat.

Our confidence level continued to rise. Stollmeyer, Rae, Christiani, and Gomez were in good form, all at the same time, and Marshall, who was also scoring heavily in County matches, could not make the Test side. Frank was also in the mood to punish the counties. I well remember an event that reveals a great deal about his character, his generosity to friends, his sense of history and occasion, and at the same time his love and respect for the culture of the game.

We were playing against Leicesteshire and the two of us came together at the crease. It was one of those days when, after playing the first over, I saw everything. I was tracking the ball, easily observing its movement, and my legs were early in position. I had a little more time that day and my timing was spot on. Everything was getting in place, and as we used to say in the BCL I was seeing the ball like a breadfruit. Frank noted this, and while we were both sticklers for tight defense, technique and methods, he noticed that the extra time I had was enabling me to place perfectly all my aggressive shots. Now this is a man that knows all about these things, and he understood what was happening because he was frequently in that state of mind and body.

When I got to about 20 or so, he came up to me in the middle and said, 'little man, in this mood you can score the fastest hundred in the season' and set tongues wagging. Of course he was aware that my style was generally in the direction of caution, and the thought of risking my hand by doing something rash was just not my style. But he saw that I was playing strokes in the approved fashion and that my legs, hands, shoulders, and eyes were talking to each other. Then he said, 'I will give you the strike and you should go for it.' That was exactly what he did, and I went for it. He would push a single and get me up to the other end to face five balls in each over.

Well, I did set up the season's record by hitting the 100 in 65 minutes. It was an exciting moment because I knew that the fellows back home would not believe I was up in England swiping, which was not my nature. They couldn't say that the bowling was sweet, because the county team was well established and respectable. So I conclude that they could only say that Weekes was getting hungrier by the week and that the little man had gone back to the BCL days when he used to confront bowling if the groove was on.

When I went in to bat on the first day, Frank was already 150 or more. I scored 25 runs in the first 35 minutes, so when Frank spoke to me I wondered why he wanted me to up gear for no apparent reason. By the end of play on the first day we were still batting; he was on 230 and I on 190. The skipper decided to let me bat on to get a double hundred. The next day I went out with Frank and it took me 40 minutes to get the required 10 runs. Frank deliberately took the strike for himself. It was his way of protesting the captain's decision which he thought would kill the game.

Frank felt that I was accustomed to scoring double hundreds and that another one at that moment was no big deal. He was convinced that Goddard should have declared the innings, and press for a team victory. So it took me 65 minutes to get a hundred and 40 minutes to get 10 runs. I believe he was of the opinion that the game had fallen into vanity, and he wanted no part of it. I read it as a vote of confidence in me. When he urged and facilitated the first hundred it was his leadership ability coming to the fore.

Frank may very well have been drawing upon reports he had received about the double century I had scored earlier in the year against British Guiana at Kensington. It was an interesting event because British Guiana had at that time the fastest bowler in the West Indies, a chap by the name of John Trim. He was certainly faster than Hinds Johnson, who was quick. But he got a flogging in that game because in addition to my 236, Roy Marshall, our elegant, stylist opener, scored a polished 191. Trim bowled 21 overs, got no wickets and conceded 110 runs. Barbados rattled up 686 for 6 declared, and defeated British Guiana by an innings and 110 runs. People said it was the same 110 runs that Trim had served up.

When the West Indies team was declared for the tour to England Trim was not included, despite his obvious pace. The selection of Johnson, Jones and Pierre almost led to a riot in Georgetown. It was the second time I was mixed up in a selection dispute because some British Guiana critics thought that my 236 was a deliberate attempt on my part to kill off Trim's Test prospect. They felt very strongly about it. Hinds Johnson, they said, was a 40 year old man, but Trim was not far behind at 35 and was yet to make his Test debut.

A newspaper in British Guiana took up the case and presented it as another example of Barbadian discrimination against British Guiana players. The 30 year old R.J Christiani was the only Guyanese player on the 1950 team, and this added fuel to the fire as these were four Barbadians, including the captain, three Jamaicans, and three Trinidadians. The newspaper carried a headline: 'Small Islands Dominate', an announcement that inflamed local passions.

We won the fourth Test at the Oval by an innings and 56 runs. The team was now in stride and proving itself superior by quite a distance. We were playing excellent cricket, and the boys appeared invincible. England had no answer to our charge.

We had the superior technology in batting and bowling, and we were pressing home our advantage. Mindful that we had defeated them 2-0 at home in 1948, we were consolidating our status as the better team in all environments.

In our first innings Rae and Frank piled up centuries, 109 and 138 respectively. Rae had scored just 14 and 10 in the first Test, but had smashed 106 in the second. In the third he got good starts with 68 and 46 not out. He was in form, and this was his second century. But Frank was merciless. After scoring 261 at Trent Bridge he piled on the agony on English bowlers with another stylish innings of 138. Clyde and I scored 17 and 30 respectively, and a captain knock from Goddard of 58 not out saw us safely to another commanding total of 503.

When England came to the crease it was really a one man show. Hutton was back! And boy, did he show his class! He ground out an innings of 202 from a total of 344; a truly majestic and historic performance. The next highest total was made by new-comer Denis Compton who made 44 run out. The damage again was done by Val who picked up 4 for 121 from 64 overs, but this time he shared the honors with Goddard who took 4 for 25 from 17 overs. Asked to follow on, a demoralized England team could muster a meagre 103, with a highest score of 29 by David Sheppard. Val again was the main wrecker; 6 for 39 from 26 overs, as repetitive a performance as an assault weapon.

It was all over. We had won the series 3-1, an improvement on the 2-0 inflicted in the Caribbean. It was the first time we had defeated the English in England and we were aware of the implications of the victory in terms of its history and politics. It was the end of Empire as far as we were concerned. London Bridge had fallen down. I had never before seen such complete mastery of an opponent in a Test series. The 48 home series and the 49 tour to India were closely fought. This tour turned out rather one-sided, largely because of the batting power we had in our deep line-up, and the mystery of Ram and Val. They struggled to penetrate our batting and Ram and Val cut through them like a hot knife in butter.

Our batting power had grown at a phenomenal rate. The 3Ws had made our debut two tours before, and this was Frank's second tour. In addition, Rae and Stollmeyer were established as the best opening pair in the world, and Goddard had proven a valuable all-rounder in the middle. Clyde was no doubt the best wicket keeper batsman in the game. He alone seemed to be able to pick Ram and Val. His keeping was excellent on tour.

At the time it was difficult to gauge how the English boys took the defeat off the field. Socially we didn't know them very well. It was in later years that a chap would invite you to a pub and discuss the tour. In those years there was informal contact. I didn't know where any of the English players lived because I was not invited to their homes. Nothing changed over the next eight years of my Test career. In fact relations soured after the 1950 defeat, and in 1954 when England toured the West Indies there were some ugly scenes and the tour was marred by rancour.

In 1957 things had changed and we got to know some of the English chaps very well. Most of them were decent men, and I would say that David Sheppard, (later Bishop and the Lord Sheppard) was the finest Englishmen I have ever met, and there were some very fine men playing cricket. I would say, also, that David was a first rate human being. We first met during the Cambridge game in 1950. He made 200 against us and we got on beautifully. Peter May was also a very fine gentleman, and a very good cricketer.

These were chaps who respected what we had done for cricket, and were prepared to concede that we were the better team. They were also prepared to engage us in discussion about the special features of our game. It is always the mark of a fine player and sportsman when he recognizes that he can learn from other players who had shown a higher standard.

We had learnt the game upon the basis of English methods and techniques. We embraced the English manual, making some important adjustments along the way in order to suit our temperament and temperature. In the process we produced something that was recognized by the world as an excellent contribution. It was not a question of boasting about our success. It was that we had done something special against the odds and we wanted recognition for it. We found that only decent fellows were willing to be fair and generous in this regard, and that is how we rated them.

We found greater acceptance among the younger players like Peter May and Colin Cowdrey. Colin was at Oxford at the time, and he made 50 against us. He was a teenager when he started in the big game. He had a lot of respect for our style, and he would ask questions. He was a part of a new and more generous breed. They would ask us how to read Ram and Val, and we would discuss techniques and methods. In 1957 they scored a lot of runs against us, by using the pad against Ram and Val. We couldn't have told them this because it was not within our culture to use the pad instead of the bat.

May and Cowdrey were natural players with a lot of talent. They were bright young men who were smart enough to realize the value of our modification to the English rules in order to produce a more aggressive, entertaining approach to batting, fielding and bowling. They realized that we were creative but yet orthodox, and they were prepared to adopt some of our approaches. In the end May and Cowdrey won a lot of West Indian fan support because of their stylish stroke play and aggression. They were willing to risk being less orthodox. What they did in 1957, and after, was entirely unorthodox.

Batting in my view is about hitting the ball where there is no fieldsman. If you are very orthodox you are going to hit the ball to the fieldsman because they are bowling with that sort of field where you would hit the ball and there would be several maiden overs bowled. That's what they want you to do, of course. But you have to be innovative; you have to be able to create space for your mind and body because if you can pick up the ball early enough you can hit it anywhere, anyhow, because you are free. Once you get to the pitch of it you are free, and freedom is also about using existing rules in order to do things differently.

An example of this is how to beat the field without hitting the ball in the air. I did not like the idea of hitting the ball in the air. In fact I have only struck one six in my Test career, and it was not intended. I hit Bill Johnson, the Australian medium fast bowler, over mid-on, off the back foot, slightly against the swing. It turned out to be a no-ball, so I would have been safe. This was a game in Trinidad in the 1955 tour in which Clyde got hundreds in each innings, and I score one in the first. In the second innings he gave it away due to exhaustion leaving me stranded on 60. The game was drawn, but I thought if he had stayed I would have made another hundred as well. I ended up with 87 not out.

After we had won the last Test at the Oval so convincingly,

the press was in awe of our team. Some journalists seemed in shock, because we were not given much credit on arrival even though we had won the previous series and had defeated India in India. In those days the English media had difficulty referring to the West Indian X1 as a team. When the word team was used they did not expect the West Indians to be included. We were just West Indians calypso entertainers, and stuff like that.

Then the party started. Some 100,000 West Indians were already in England, recently arrived and having a difficult time with jobs, housing, and racism. They were looking to us to lighten their daily burden, and they flocked to the grounds hoping we would lift their spirits and restore the pride daily stripped away from their lives. They brought musical instruments and we could hear the sound of the West Indies pouring out of the stands during the games.

It lifted our spirits as well, and for sure I enjoyed the atmosphere created. The animated sound of the crowd was always important to me. The calypso singers had a wonderful time, singing familiar tunes, and creating new ones, such as the now famous "Cricket lovely Cricket" by Lord Beginner and Lord Kitchener.

It was all very appropriate because sections of the British press had berated us on arrival. After we won our first Test, they described us as a bunch of calypsonians. It was difficult in my view to see why they couldn't see us as a competitive team. We bowled well, fielded well, and won matches.

So while we got some respect from the players the media were not so generous.

There were exceptions, of course, because writers like Jim Swanton and Neville Cardus wrote fairly of our efforts. In fact, they were very literate men, who became converts to the

West Indies brand of cricket, and did so for the rest of their lives. Cardus wrote a piece in which he referred to me as the new Bradman and Frank as the new Ponsford. This was a compliment because not only were these men rated the best in the world for their time, but when the West Indies were last in Australia in 1930/31, they had put us to the sword. In the first Test Ponsford struck 92 not out, and 183 in the second. In the third Test he was at it again with 109, and joined by Don with 223; In the fourth Test the Don continued with 152.

This was a comforting commentary from someone who was paying attention and was generous in judgment. The public, however, welcomed and celebrated our display. They liked the quality of what they saw and celebrated the fact that we had played in the finest spirit of the game we all loved. They saw in us a little of Learie Constantine whom they admired. Learie was living in England and was a great source of inspiration to us.

Learie, furthermore, was a kind patron; he looked after our many needs. In 1949 in India when I scored the fifth Test hundred I received a cable from him that was very warm in terms of the language used. I didn't receive one from the WICBC, which made his the more valuable to me. But in 1950, he did say to us that our victory signaled the 'end of empire', the moment he had long cherished.

EIGHT

FIRST NUMBER ONE
WORLD RATING, 1950

BY THE END OF THE 1950 TOUR there were two significant developments in West Indies cricket. Both on reflection were important milestones. One of these was personal, but from a public perspective meant a great deal for our cricket. The second was literary and political, and spoke to our maturity as a cricket nation. These developments overlapped and represented where we had reached since Test status was granted in 1927.

The first of these was that by the end of the summer I was being rated the number one batsman in the world by cricket statisticians and pundits. This assessment was based on my short but productive journey into the Test arena, and general views about my methods and techniques. I was not one to focus on such evaluations. In any event I was of the opinion that Frank was the best batsman we had. This is how it played out in my mind. Frank was brilliant, and Clyde, when he got going, was the most destructive batting force imaginable.

The statistic was used by those who had time to count and to assess. I was so busy focusing on getting more runs, of which I never felt I had made enough. There was always this sense with me that I could not be satisfied with the tally thus far. The thirst was deep and I wanted more, a lot more. The five consecutive centuries were fine, but five is a smaller number than ten. A batsman's greed may or may not be a good thing but I wanted to see the West Indies team rated as unbeatable.

I knew that the 1950 team was the beginning of a new dispensation. Earlier teams did not do very well between the wars. We lost 3-0 in our inaugural 1928 tour in England, and tied the return home tour 1-1 in 1930. We toured Australia in 1930/31 and lost 4-1. We returned to England in 1933 and lost 3-0, but won the return series 2-1 in 1934. Our last series, before the war broke was our tour to England in the summer of 1939 which England won 1-0.

The postwar team was a new beginning and the 3Ws were at the centre of the rebirth. Winning the 1948 series against England in the West Indies, and the 1949 series in India, followed by victory in 1950, placed us on the cusp of world dominance. We were on a winning streak and most of us had never been a part of a losing Test team. There was a very real sense of being unbeatable, and to be a part of this state of affairs was unbelievable.

After 1950, I could not have imagined that we would fall. Rather, I imagined that we would go on to become the best side in the world. If this was to happen, then I would have to continue batting as I did in India, and Frank and Clyde would have to bat as they did in England, and so on. We only had the Aussies to take care of and we would have been the undisputed leaders of world cricket. Our team was learning to be consistent.

It looked as solid as it was possible to imagine. Meanwhile, the pundits were looking at my performance statistics and making comparative judgments.

By the end of the tour I had played in 13 Test matches in just under two years. The matches and scores were as follows:

1948 vs. England in West Indies:
1st Test: 35 and 25...................... 60
2nd Test: 36 and 20................... 56
3rd Test: 36.............................. 36
4th Test:141.............................. 141

1949 vs. India in India
1st Test: 128............................. 128
2nd Test: 194............................. 194
3rd Test: 162 and 101............... 263
4th Test; 90............................. 90
5th Test: 56 and 48................... 104

1950 vs. England in England
1st Test: 52 and 1...................... 53
2nd Test: 63 and 63................... 126
3rd Test: 129............................ 129
4th Test: 30............................. 30
Total:.................................... 1,410
Average:................................ 74

I had scored six centuries in nineteen innings from 13 Tests, and I was 25 years old. The experts concluded that my average of 74 was phenomenal, and that no batsman in the world had such an average at that time. I took the comments in stride.

Sure it was good to have scored the runs at such a rate. But I was thinking of winning more games for the West Indies, and seeing other players perform well.

Scoring 1,410 runs at an average of 74 after just three tours, batting at nos. 3 and 4, was my way of expressing commitment to West Indies cricket, and at the same time securing my future as a sportsman who had no other way of securing an adequate income. I lived in constant awareness of my weak financial condition. The insecurity this bred was something which Frank and I discussed on more than one occasion. It was certainly the reason we turned professional and played in the English Leagues. Some of us would have preferred to play in the more prestigious County circuit but the opportunities were not readily available.

My entry into the English League in order to make a living that was not provided by playing for the West Indies was the only serious option available to those of us with a less than secure financial background. At the same time it was an excellent opportunity to hone our skills. There was no need for team mates like Stollmeyer or Goddard to follow this path because they were men of substantial means and relatively easy access to public resources. But we were in the same team and we had to play as a team even in the face of extreme inequality in our financial conditions.

I was ranked the number one batsman in the world but it had no meaningful impact upon my financial condition. If Coopers and Lybrand had also conducted an audit of my finances they probably would have found that I was ranked the poorest senior batman in the world. Maybe Ram was similarly disposed, coming as he did from the labouring class of rural Trinidad, but even then I am told his family had a few acres of land on which he could farm and make a living. Frank was acutely aware of this problem and was determined to break out. So he was first to turn professional, and then to enter university, and so on. But he was blessed with high social skills in addition to his cricket intelligence. Also, he was supremely confident in his ability and would have challenged anyone who sought to impose on him an injustice. He was not always tolerant of silly situations, and I respected him for this.

I had emerged from the Bridgetown poor, and by force of hard work, a focused mind, a scientific approach to my craft, I reached a position which the experts said was the top of the world. What did it mean? Well, for sure I was not in a position to do much about it. I certainly did not know how to convert my enormous status into property, and the WICB, my employer, was not interested in fostering such a transition. The Board was in the hands of the rich and powerful in the region and saw players such as myself in a way that estate owners saw field hands. We were called to work, received a stipend on which we could not live, given a uniform that made us look the part, and when the job was done we were sent packing until required for the next year's crop. This might seem an exaggeration, but it best explains the reality in which I found myself, and those team-mates of similar background.

I had no doubt that if any day my form was weakened and runs dried up, I would be on the skid without a period of recovery. Maybe this condition served to focus my mind even more, but it generated considerable anxiety. I was not one of the elite boys, and I certainly felt that given the way they treated Frank in 1949, and after, that I would have received even shorter words. After all, Frank was considered one of the players with a good education background who was able to chart his own independent path outside of cricket. I was dependent, and therefore more vulnerable. There were many administrators, and a few team-mates, who wanted us to feel that way.

It was no simple matter working in this environment. It required considerable mental toughness and personal discipline. It was easy to become distracted and lose sight of what was really critical, which was serving West Indies cricket. There were legends like Constantine and Headley who were counting on me. They had gone through even greater challenges with the early colonial set up, and the race and class hostility. They were never given the kind of respect by officials inside the region compared with what they had received outside.

I was in danger of being affected by the same plight. Outside the West Indies officials were prepared to open doors for me, and at home people were busy trying to close them. It was a strange predicament, but I had the good fortune of being able to think these things through and to see the tree from the forest. There was a lot of competition for spaces in the Barbados line-up. Frank went to Jamaica, and Gary Sobers joined us. Good players were on the outside watching and waiting for a chance. Tragically, we were getting ready to lose Roy Marshall.

The second development was meeting C.L.R. James. He had not yet written his famous book, 'Beyond a Boundary', this came after the 1957 tour, but he was writing in the English newspapers, and Frank especially used to read his columns and talk about his ideas and opinions on our cricket. He was greatly inspired by what we had done on the tour. He was a close friend of Learie, and was an admirer of Headley. He knew the English players and was close to Neville Cardus. He wrote that he had never seen before cricket such as what we had played.

James made two points that gripped my attention: that we

West Indians had saved cricket for the world, because the English after the War seemed hell-bent on playing a dull, anti-social version of the game which he thought would destroy its mass appeal; second, that we had brought drama, elegance, and gentlemanly values back into the game. He also thought that with the 3 Ws it would be difficult to bowl out the West Indies twice, cheaply. He was a believer in having a good opening pace attack, and considered this our weakness. He was of the opinion that Ram and Val needed protection, and the seamers we had in Gomez and Goddard could not provide it. He didn't think they were first class. He was a very insightful critic.

James came to the hotel and invited Frank and I for a meal. I don't know why just the two of us. He knew Frank well from his Manchester days. We had dinner, and talked more about politics than cricket. He introduced me to the state of West Indian politics. We discussed the idea of Federation in a serious way. He had attended the leadership conference in Montego Bay. He thought that Frank had some very good qualities, and that these were necessary to lead the West Indies team as a public institution in the cause of regional integration. He was very strong on the point that the cricket team should be the flagship of the Federation.

James also stressed that West Indian people were ready to manage their own affairs, and that our victory over England was the kind of proof required to convince non-believers. He spoke about wanting independence within a Federation, and stated that cricket was the key. That I hailed from a working class background made me a special candidate in his eyes, being a confirmed socialist. But he liked Frank, and thought he was the best man to lead the transition from colonial to nationalist cricket in the West Indies.

He was a brilliant man, and this was clear from just listening to him. He spoke about people and issues that I had never heard about. He had the ability to put over complex issues in clear language. I felt he was getting ready to say something major about West Indies cricket, and we were being scouted out. Importantly, I knew he wanted the players to realize there was a bigger purpose behind our cricket. He watched our social habits and assessed our state of mind. He was looking beyond the cricket. He was looking for a political statesman.

Frank stated that he was interested in what he called my intellectual bent of mind. He would say that no one could play the way I do without a mental arrangement that suggests a high sort of intellect. I had no idea what he meant but I could only tell him that reading the game was the first call of a batsman. He was a great believer in that, and figured that it is how you order your thoughts that explained how you act on them. He admired Frank, and so did I. This made us friends.

Frank's average on the tour was in excess of my own, an excellent performance for a man that had not played Test cricket in near two years. Winning the Lord's Test gave us immense personal pleasure. It has remained the high point in my cricketing career. We wanted to win. We were a mixed race team, the only one of its kind in Test cricket, Indians, blacks, whites, Jews, Portuguese, we had everything. We played well because we wanted to win. It meant so much to us, and to West Indian people everywhere.

NINE

SECOND NUMBER ONE WORLD RATING, 1956

I ENTERED THE 1950S ON TOP OF MY GAME
and exited with my Test career ended and questions were being
asked whether I pulled out or was pushed. The latter events
surrounded my last series, the momentous 1958 Pakistan tour
of the West Indies. I have often been asked whether I retired or
was 'made' to retire. After the Pakistan tour I retired formally
from Test cricket. I got to the stage where I was not enjoying
it as much as I did in previous years. I thought I had set a fairly
high standard and to maintain it entailed considerable work. I
was then 33; still young in body, but the mind had aged.

There were some additional issues, I must admit, that brought
forward the actual moment of my retirement. Specifically, I
refer to some remarks that were made by Cecil DeCaires, one
of our officials, after we were defeated in 1957 in England. He
did not speak very kindly of Clyde and myself when we
returned home after losing the series. His remarks to the press

were unkind and not true. We did not do well in England, and I will say a few things about that, but the statements from management created an untenable situation.

One of the items reported was that Clyde and I did not make a serious attempt to get fit on the tour. This was quite untrue, and speaking of my own case, the nature of my medical problem was not appreciated. I reported the pain I was enduring, and in the end had to undergo five surgical procedures for sinusitis. My team mates made jokes that my blocked sinuses made me snore like a guinea pig. I had very serious problems breathing on the field, and sleeping at night. Significantly, I had acute headaches and my vision was sometimes blurred, a very serious condition for a batsman, especially one of my kind who depended more on touch than power.

I was told later that the Queen had the same medical procedures from a gentleman named Mr. Hogg in Harley Street. I had my punctures just before she did. The procedures were not very complicated. They inserted an instrument into the sinuses and cleared the channels. I had a very serious case. When I saw Mr. Hogg he thought I should not be out there playing at all because he was sure I was having signs of double vision. I panicked a little when I heard that because a bowler hasn't got to be really quick to take life. The skipper, however, thought that even in my sick condition, as on the Australian tour 1951–52 when I pulled a muscle in the first Test match, I should play. In fact his words were: 'with one leg Everton you are still good enough to play as well as some of the other chaps with two legs.'

After the 1950 success in England we were perhaps the most confident cricket team on the planet. Twice in a row we defeated England, in our backyard and in theirs. In between these assignments, we had honed our batting skills against the Indian in the length and breath of the massive country. When we got to Australia, there was a sense in the camp that we did not know what to expect because we did not know the chaps we were playing against. We knew them by reputation, but West Indies had not played the Aussies since the 1930s. We wanted to square the history because we had never defeated them; but we were on a roll. If we had swept them along with the tide, we would have been rated world camps, so to speak. It was a time of great expectation.

Things did not work out in Australia as we had imagined and planned. We were sure that Ram and Val would do well, and that we would get runs. But of concern was our pace attack, as it was in England. Since we knew little about their players, I did wonder what the absence of a balanced attack would mean. We took Jones, and Trim got his chance. But I thought our reliance on Frank and Gerry Gomez as seamers, and occasionally Goddard, could see us through. What I had not factored was the real pace of the Aussie attack, led by Ray Lindwall and Keith Miller, and ably supported by W. A. Johnston. They were quick, no doubt about it and they gave us more than a little trouble, especially at the top of the order.

We lost the warm up match against Queensland, a bad sign in itself, but my spirits were not daunted. In fact, when we turned up at Brisbane for the first Test we had put that event behind us, and were prepared for battle. And we did get one, which we lost but should have won. We made countless mistakes in the field, and let the Aussies off the hook. We stayed in the leadership of most matches until the final stages. These were the toughest games I had played. It was like a toe to toe heavy weight boxing contest in which no one flinched but the one that made the final, fatal error fell to the canvas.

We won the toss and chose to bat. It was our first chance to experience the Aussie pace. The press hyped the series in terms of West Indies spin versus Aussie pace. It was ranked as the showdown for world leadership in Test cricket. The experts were saying whichever attack was more lethal would walk away with the world title. We did not play a pacer, and there was no reason why we should have worried about their spinner, D.T. Ring.

In the first over Rae was bowled by Lindwall without a score on the board. He was completely beaten for pace. Michael Manley wrote in his book, '*The History of West Indies Cricket*', that Rae's stumps were knocked back before he had properly raised the bat. There is much truth in this statement. The delivery was quick and Rae was not yet in position. The crowd went wild. Frank went in at number three, and settled things down, but not before Johnston had sent back Stollmeyer for 8, leaving us on 18 for 2.

It was a disastrous start. I joined Frank at the crease in the midst of this frenzy. We did our best to calm the storm, adding some 40 runs before Frank was bowled by Johnston. Christiani and I added another 30 runs before I was caught off Ring for 35. The skipper, Goddard, did very well coming in at no.9 and top-scoring with 45 in a modest total of 216. Lindwall bowled magnificently ending with 4 for 62 from 20 overs. I thought I handled the pace pretty well, and falling to the spinner was a bit of a disappointment because I had built up my mind to dig in for a big score. I was not daunted, and thought we could defend the total.

What a game it was. It had everything of the making of a great Test match. The Aussies went in, started slowly, cautiously, and then began to crumble. How they got to 226 was entirely our fault. We dropped so many catches! It was as if we didn't want to dominate. Frank and Gomez opened the bowling, and didn't do too badly. But the skipper was keen to get them off, rough up the ball, and bring on our heavy ammunition. Val was the man who ripped through the batting, picking up 5 for 99 from 25 overs, while Ram, as an excellent partner, picked up one for 75 from 24 overs. Gerry and Frank came on at the end and rapped up the tail. Had not for some cultivated swinging of the bat from Lindwall batting at no. 7, the score would have been much less. He swung the blade and racked up 61, the top score, in short time.

At least we knew, that despite our poor fielding, the Aussies would struggle against Ram and Val, as did the English. Rae and Stollmeyer gave us a better start in the second innings, but once again, we dug ourselves into a bit of a hole. We saw off the pace attack of Miller and Lindwall, just to allow leg spinner Ring to take 6 for 80, wrecking our performance. I remember being determined to resist with a mixture of counter attack and defense. In the end I topped scored with 70. It wasn't easy out there but I felt up to it, and my form was good. *Wisden* carried a headline which said "Weekes dominate the Australian attack striking hard and fluently". Well, there was some truth in that, because I knew I had to take the challenge to Lindwall and Miller, and to create room for Ram and Val to operate.

My 70 runs inning was a tough affair. I went back to base rules and deployed the methods and techniques that had served me well in the past; using the feet, back and across to counter the pace and to be in a position to punish the short balls and drive the over-pitched. I was bombarded with bouncers. I can't remember how many there were but they came fast and furious.

I was targeted for a bumber bombardment. I knew how to handle myself. As a little man my lower body movement was brisk which gave me the advantage in terms of positioning my upper body. Technically, I was prepared to deal with the encounter, and felt it was only a matter of time before I got into the big runs. We secured a total of 245 which gave the Aussies a target of 236 runs to win.

The skipper did what he had done in England during the Oval Test. He rubbed the new ball into the ground, after Gomez and Frank had bowled three overs. It did not matter that Gomez had taken out opener Archer for 4 when the score was on 8. The purpose of the action was to get Ram and Val into the act as soon as possible. It might have been a good strategy because Ram, this time, picked up 5 for 90 from 40 overs. Val also bowled 40 overs, but picked up just 1 wicket for 117.

In the end the Aussies got home with three wickets to spare, with Morris top scoring on 48. The 80 overs bowled between Ram and Val were excessive, and revealed our over-dependence on them. It might seem strange that the two openers bowled just 5 overs and the spinners 80. The tactics used by the skipper were described by the critics as lacking imagination, and unfair on all bowlers. Frank, after all, had bowled 2 overs for 2 runs, and Gomez 3 overs, taking 1 for 12. Val's 40 overs for 1 wicket might seem difficult to comprehend today but with Ram and Val bowling there was always an expectation.

I was seriously injured during the match. In the Australian second innings I pulled a leg muscle fielding in the slips. There was enormous pain and deep disappointment. I was a professional cricketer and of course carried on playing. Every morning I got a needle inserted into the leg and this was very painful. I was told at the time that the doctor was using needles normally set aside for race horse. The pain interfered tremendously with my mobility. I still believe we should have won that match, and if we did the rest of the tour could have been very different. We batted and bowled well but our fielding was awful. This is where we fell. In one spell, at least five catches went down off Val, which explained in part why the skipper kept him going. It was a poor performance in the field that caused us the game, and a bite at history.

The second Test was in many ways the turning point of the series. We went to Sydney where I knew the wicket would be hard, fast, and bouncy. For this reason we left out the extra batsman, Roy Marshall, and brought in Jones to open the bowling. Australia won the toss and put us in thinking that Miller and Lindwall would run us through in short time. This did not happen. We had a series of good performances, no century, but a few fifties that gave us a good score of 362. Lindwall did get four wickets, including mine, bowled for 5. But Frank (64), Clyde(60), Christiani (76) and Gomez (54) saw us through. There were a few good partnerships during the innings that suggest we were not in any serious trouble on the pitch.

Disaster struck when the Aussies went in to bat. The hard, bouncy surface reduced the turn that Ram was accustomed to getting with the leg spin. The result was that batsmen could push down the line and play without having their edges broken off. They would push down the line, play for a little turn, and wait for the over-pitched delivery. Skipper Hassett and Miller exploited the conditions to full effect. They neutralized Ram and racked up big innings -Hassett, 132 and Miller, 129. Ram, for the first time, bowled his heart out without reward, and appeared tired and broken. He sent down 41overs and conceded

143 runs without a wicket. Val, on the other hand, bowled less, but still considerably, and picked up 4 for 111 from his 31 overs. Posting 517, and with Ram mastered for the first time in his career, and on the retreat, I knew that it was a crossroads in the series.

Despite my pain, I pressed on and keeping Lindwall and Miller at bay, scored 56 in an innings of 290. The skipper top scored with just one more run, but ran out of partners as the tail offered no resistance. With just under 140 to win, the Aussies walked home with seven wickets in hand. It was a painful game, both mentally and physically. The 'horse doctor', some of the chaps jokingly called the physicians who tended to my leg, did not get my pain to go away completely. This could have been done but I would not have had any sensation in my hand to hold the bat. I knew that my legs were slower in response, and I tried to compensate by moving a little earlier. This worked to some extent and I got runs, but the pain was tearing away at my concentration, and each run seemed harder than the previous one.

At the Adelaide Oval we received showers of blessings. Heavy rains had affected the wicket, and yet, Australia who had won the toss, opted to bat. Frank was excellent, and bowling his medium slow seamers, got the ball to swing through the air and dip late causing havoc for the batsmen. It is fair to say that Frank was unplayable on the pitch. He was always a fine seamer, and with the slightest support, could devastate. He picked up 6 for 38 from 12 overs, claiming both openers. The top scorer made 23, and Goddard, also with his seamers, picked up three and Gomez one. The services of Ram and Val were not required. No pacer was included and Denis Atkinson, also a seamer, was selected in his place.

When our turn to bat came, it seemed like more of the same. Collapsing at 3 for 34, in good sunlight I went to the wicket, bandaged leg, but determined to fight to the end. We were bundled out for a mere 105, and once again topped score with an inadequate total. On this occasion it was 26, a long, gritty, miserable looking 26 that many writers have spoken about as the lowest match winning innings in a four innings Test. I was not bothered about that. I was more concerned that having decided to deal positively with the pace of Miller and Lindwall I had fallen three times to Johnston, the medium pacer, and twice bowled. Thanks to a fine spell from Val, 6 for 102, we restricted the Aussies to 255. By now the pitch had dried out and was playing quite well. Ram continued to slide. Maybe his confidence was falling, and he seemed less menacing as the tour progressed. We were left with 233 to win, and smelling victory all the chaps stuck in and reached the total with six wicket in hand.

The series was not over. We were back in there with a chance, and feeling good about the win, enthusiasm was rekindled. As it turned out we were well on course to win at Melbourne, and as the critics have said, we gave it away. The skipper took the flack, but as in any game, it could have tilted in the other direction. We won the toss and batted. Frank was back to his excellent self. He wasn't in full fitness, nursing a hand injury. He scored the first century of the tour for us, a stylish 108 before he was bowled by Lindwall. I fell for 1, but the middle order notched up a few modest scores and we reached 272. Miller picked up 5 for 60, an interesting sign because we had selected Trim for the first time of the series. When the Aussies went in to bat Trim got stuck in; with a fast spell picked up 5 for 34 from 12 overs.

The Aussies were reduced to 216. It did make me wonder about the Trim episode in British Guiana a few years back. We were all out for 203 in the second innings, and I, adding just one more to the one I scored in the first innings, thought that the 260 Australia had to win would be a serious challenge. With nine wickets down, and Val with 5, the score was 223. Who could have imagined that the last pair, in this critical match, nos. 9 and 11, could have made it to 260? But they did. The media made a meal of the skipper's field placing. Trying to pick up the last wicket he brought in the field in an attacking mode while the batsmen were swinging their bats and the ball was somehow dropping behind our heads and generally eluding our grasp. The Aussie tail lived to tell the tale of how it denied us victory and claim for its team an unassailable 3-1 lead in the series. Val picked up his third five wicket haul, but to no celebratory avail.

The fifth Test ran much like the third, a low scoring affair, in which Gomez and Frank repeated their devastation of the Aussies. Gomez picked up seven and Frank three leaving a total of 116. We could not improve upon this performance, and were out for 78. I added nothing to the score, and was again back in Lindwall's ledger. The Aussies replied with 377. We were all out for 213, Stollmeyer scoring our second century, and handing the Aussies victory by 202 runs. The dream of our world supremacy had suffered a serious setback. The bubble was burst, and we returned rather deflated to the West Indies licking our wounds. It was a case of things going wrong that should have been arrested. We did not deserve the 3-1 defeat. We allowed things to slip from our grasp after we had done the hard work. We had only ourselves to blame for losing matches we should have won. A golden opportunity was dashed.

I do believe had I not been seriously injured events might have been different. I was in form when the tour started, and had developed a command of the Aussie attack. It has been said that Miller and Lindwall were the undoing of the West Indies. There is some truth in that and the statistics show this. But what they do not show is that Frank, Clyde and I were all seriously injured at different times. There is no doubt that they were fine bowlers, some of the best in the business, and for sure the fastest I had played in my Test career. But the 3Ws were there, and with a little help from nature the results could have been a little different.

I was a sad man leaving Australia. I had looked forward to the contest, the opportunity to test my skills against the finest opposition available at that time. The Aussies got the upper hand, and as you know they are never prepared to let it go when they have it. But I learnt a great deal on the tour about playing conditions and the range of players available to Australian selectors. My focus shifted to getting fit again as soon as possible in order to redress the tour imbalance.

But there was not much time. We were soon rushing off to New Zealand for a two match Test series. The pain was still there in my leg, and in my heart. New Zealand would not be the catharsis I was looking for. Some players saw the tour as preparation for the upcoming arrival of the Indians in the West Indies. My preference was always to see each Test team as the hardest and play them accordingly. Cricket is filled with surprises, and if you offer it disrespect, it will jump up like a bad dog and bite you.

In the first Test at Christ Church, it was Ram and Val back into the attack. They bowled out our host for 236 and we in turn did only marginally better thanks to a classic partnership between Frank (71) and Clyde (65). Ram and Val once again scuttled the host for a mere 189 and we cruised to victory with Frank carrying his bat for 62. The second Test ended in a draw but we were able to mount a display for the thousands who turned up of good West Indian batting. The openers did very well. Rae fell one short of his century but Stollmeyer continued for 152. Then the 3Ws moved in and did the rest. Frank struck an even century, Clyde 115, and I held up the base with 51. The massive total of 546 exhausted the time available for the match to end in any team's favor.

In a sense, then, the short tour to New Zealand provided a confidence boost that was much required. They were not a bad team. We had been tested against the Australians and had lifted our game during the disastrous experience. As a middle order, the 3Ws were just beginning to feel its full potential. I felt that along the way other teams would pay. Frank was in excellent form and Clyde, still feeling the effects of carrying the gloves, was improving his Test game daily.

I focused on building the mind aspects of my game, and became a better batsman after Australia. I had been tested by excellent spin in India, superb swing bowling in England, and sheer pace in Australia. My game was raised several notches. I knew it each time I walked to the wicket in New Zealand. By the time we got home and started the tour against India my game was probably at its best. The process of refinement was well advanced, and poor India, it was their turn again.

I was not picking on India. It was the turn of the tide. The first match was played in Trinidad. Some people were already saying that it was my favourite ground on account of the amount of runs I have scored there. Maybe there was a relationship. What I will say is that some pitches and grounds do have a special feel, and maybe Queens Park Oval suits my temperament. India won the toss and batted, and did pretty well scoring 417 after P.R. Umrigar played an excellent innings of 130. The thirst for runs, and something more, within our team, after the battering from the Aussies, was evident. In those days chaps would say things like, 'I am going to slaughter these fellows today', and would go out and do it.

I was not worried about their magic spinner, S.P Gupte. The rumors were that he was unplayable, and that we would not be able to pick him, and tales like that. Well, it was true that he was a master spinner; there was no doubt about that; and he did embarrass many of our chaps who tried to use their feet. But as with all spinners the key was to watch the ball out of the hand and to read it in flight. You need to be able to do these things if you wish to have an advantage. If you are a class player, you would have goods eyes, and with intense concentration you will see the turn of the wrist, the twist of the fingers, and the motion of the ball in flight. You read these signs and you are pretty well ahead of the game.

I got back into my old groove and before I knew it I was on my way to the first of two double centuries scored on the tour. I ended on 207 in the first innings, and watched with pleasure much of B.H. Pairaudeau's maiden Test century, a very important 115 that ensured we got a small lead. Ending on 438 was reassuring despite Gupte's 7 for 162. I was pleased that Clyde was not given the gloves in this match. We had brought in A.P. Binns, and Clyde's 47 was an indicator of what was to come. The match came to a tame draw, the result of some slow batting and an absence of the usual magic from Ram and Val. At this stage I began to wonder if the return to Kensington Oval would see a continuation of my 1949 Indian tale.

Barbados played an X1 against India as a prelude to the Test. This was the game in which Gary made his Barbados debut. I had the good fortune of not only playing in that match but scoring 253 while Gary picked up 7 wickets in the two innings; not bad for a kid on the home turf. We went on to win the Barbados Test by a handsome margin. In the first innings Clyde was unfortunately given out lbw on 98; I also fell short on 47 as we wobbled to 296. If the spin twin of Gupte and M.H. Mankad did the dixie it was Val's turn when the Indians went in. He was in excellent form, and picked up 4 wickets, though he bowled 41 overs for 58 runs with 21 maidens. These data speak for themselves, and suggest that his deliveries could not be struck off the square.

The 253 runs India scored gave us an opportunity to press home to victory. D.G. Phadkar had other ideas and went to work with a lovely spell of seam bowling, picking up 5 for 64, leaving us reeling on 228 all out. There was some panic in the camp. A solid performance from the Indian batsmen, as in the first Test, and we would have been up against it. But, for the first time in a while, Ram struck in the manner the world had come to expect of him, capturing 5 for 26 from 24 overs. It was the most spectacular thing to watch. Ram was on the spot, and the Indians could not get their innings going. Bundled out for 129 we won by 142 runs giving us the series lead that had eluded us in the first Test.

I ran into a better rhythm in the third Test at my old stomping ground, Queens Park Oval, striking 161 run out and 55 not out in a drawn game. The fourth Test at Bourda was also drawn, but not before Clyde romped to 125 in the first innings. Frank and I picked up half centuries, 56 and 86 respectively, in a game that again confirmed Val as the finest and most overworked spinner in the world. He ended with match figures of 8 for 198 from 87 overs.

When we finally got to Sabina Park for the fifth Test the tour had built nicely into a war of attrition, with neither side prepared to capitulate. India did well, I thought, to post a decent score of 312, especially since Val was doing his magic once again, ending with 5 for 64 from 27 overs. Umrigar dug in and played Val with growing confidence, but lacked support in the middle. Sabina Park by then had become a place where the 3Ws had grown accustomed to high performances, and we treated the Jamaicans to a favourite dish; Frank, 237, Clyde 118, and yours truly, 109. The spin twins of Gupte and Mankad did what they had to do, and picked up five each but not before we had reached 576 that gave them something much higher that the Blue mountains to climb. Their 444 reply saw the contest peter out as did the Bourda Test, but I felt the 3Ws had done a competent job in helping to put the team back on track for a second crack at world leaders.

The Indians were not the best bowling side in the world, but they arguably were the best fielding side. Gupte was special. He bowled two types of leg breaks and of course, two googlies. He disguised them all pretty well. He was the only leg-spin bowler I knew who was able to flight the ball. Normally off-spinners can do that quite easily. The ball looked to be coming at you and then it was not there. You would push forward and be left waiting. Some strange things could happen to a chap when he is left waiting in vain. I think Bob Marley wrote a song about the idea. He left a lot of people stranded in the middle and looking very untidy.

The Press made a great deal of my performance on the tour.

146

There was a report which said the Indian diet agreed with me, and wondered why. An expert said my 716 runs for the tour was a record, the largest total by one of our boys on a home tour. I believe I had made three centuries and the 161 was not out. When last I checked the statistics were showing I finished with an average of something like 102. This enabled me to maintain an average of over 100 against the Indians. But that is how it was, and the bottom line had to do with the enduring principle that you should play each ball on merit and decide on facing each as if it will be your last. You see, unless you make that decision it is highly likely that the last ball could be in your last match.

Recovering fully from injury, however, was proving to be a bit of a proposition. The leg was slow in healing with its hidden, lurking impact upon the mind. In short time the English were upon us. It would be a major challenge and I knew it; possibly greater than 1950. I felt we could beat them again, making it three in a row, but some new facts were surfacing that required our attention. The English had regained the Ashes at home, the first time in nineteen years, against the very side that had defeated us two years ago. This was big cricket news everywhere. The mighty Aussies were toppled by England.

But there were some pluses for us that could not be ignored. We had more or less the same side that defeated England in 1950, and it was more experienced and better balanced. We knew, our team, each other, a consideration that should be contrasted with the fact that in 1950 many of us were strangers to each other. Also, we had history on our side. We had never lost a home series since we started playing Test in 1928. We were not going to allow this nice piece of legacy to slip through our fingers. Defending home turf is a very serious matter in any sport, and we were sure the West Indian public was not ready to hold their heads in shame.

The media publicity said the English were bringing two brand new pacers who would run through us in the way they said Miller and Lindwall had done. The persons they were making reference to I believe were Freddie Trueman and Brian Statham. Bedser was not touring, and the hype of these two gentlemen was considerable. Of course Hutton and Evans were seasoned campaigners, very much respected. Hutton was classy, though there was some suspicion that he would rather avoid real pace. Trevor Bailey, we knew, was as hard as nails, and would burrow if he saw an opening. Hutton was given the job as captain, a decision that created considerable turmoil in some English quarters because he was the first professional to be so honoured. The anxiety soon ceased because he took the Ashes, and put out the fire, so to speak.

Stollmeyer continued as our captain. He was experienced, and had earned his place as a reliable opener. I thought it was considered a fair decision. The series soon degenerated into controversy as player relations were not the best. Frank wrote a book, 'Cricket Punch", about this matter and set out clearly what the issues were and how we should look at them. He was clear minded on the facts and I have nothing to add, other than to say this: some of us did not see a real problem because the rough and tumble of League cricket in Lancashire had prepared us to deal with the Yorkshire personalities we found in both Trueman and Hutton. In the end the series was drawn, 2-2. We kept our pride, and the English kept their prominence. They had the Ashes to keep them warm while we prepared for a real roasting by the Aussies the following year.

We won the first Test quite convincingly at Sabina Park, by

140 runs. Happily for us we won the toss and batted on a good track that enabled us to reach 417. I believe that my modest 55 helped a little, but fresher in my memory are the events that followed when J.K. Holt, the emerging local star, who batted at no. 3, was given out lbw on 94 by Jamaican umpire, Perry Burke. We almost had a riot on our hands.

Burke was placed under police protection because the crowd felt an injustice was done. In their opinion the ball struck rather high on the pad and would have climbed over the top of the stumps. Sabina Park in those days was never without a dull moment. In short time the English were all out for 170, with Ram and Val taking seven between them. It was a marathon spell of spin. They bowled 66 of the 89 overs we sent down. When it was our turn to bat the skipper, as if to provide company for Holt, declared at 209 for 6, leaving me stranded, strangely, on 90. I cannot say that I understood the cricket logic of the decision, but then again a captain is expected to have a higher grasp of such matters.

Injury kept me out of the second Test in Barbados, and after Frank failed to score in the first innings' Clyde went into hyperdrive and scored a towering 220 in a total of 383 that dug England into a very deep hole. Ram and Val did it again, taking seven wickets between them and leaving the game to go firmly in our favour. In the second innings J.K. finally came good with 166, after which the skipper declared again, this time leaving Frank on 76. When I returned for the third Test and was bowled by Tony Lock for 94 a little rumour started that I would not score a hundred in the series. We were all very impressed with Hutton's 169 in the first innings, and when England romped to victory I did wonder whether my innings had been a little too aggressive.

If ever I had lost batting confidence there was no better place to play than Queen's Park Oval. I cannot say that after scoring two nineties I was unhappy returning to the old lady of my dreams. What in fact happened was that the 3Ws got into gear and just kept rolling until we were ready to declare, without controversy, on 681 for 8. Clyde continued his form and hammered 124; Frank struck that inner cord that allowed him to dance so elegantly for 167, and I found myself languishing on 206. Thanks to splendid innings in the middle order from Peter May(135) and Denis Compton(133) England eased out from our grasp and found solace in a tame draw. I felt good about my innings because while I was not satisfied my injury was well healed, I was in a place where I could ignore it and keep the legs doing the right thing.

It was a good thing that the double at Queen's Park Oval had pleased my spirit because the final Test at Sabina Park gave me no performance pleasure. In the first innings I did not trouble the scorer, and in the second merely irritated him. But there was enormous pleasure in seeing Gary making his Test debut, picking up wickets and scoring a few runs. I was trilled when he ripped off Bailey's edge to claim his first Test victim, especially as it was the said Bailey who picked up seven of us sending the team crashing with just 139 to its name.

Gary came into the side to replace Val who was dropped, a big decision in its own right. If you are going to drop a big player with a powerful legacy it is best to replace him with a youth with similar potential. Gary was very impressive with the ball in the game. We relied on him for long spells and he did not disappoint. He got 4 wickets in the first inning and bowled something like 28 overs.

Clyde's 116 could not save us, largely because Hutton had

clinched the advantage with his captain's knock of 205. At the same time I accepted that we had drawn a series against England who had defeated the Aussies that had trounced us. I did not do too badly in the series. While my fitness was not as I would have wished, the 69 average did suggest that my form was good. Hutton and Clyde topped the batting averages with 96 and 87 respectively. But the good news was that finally, Ram was back among the wickets, picking up 22 at an average of 24 runs each.

I had pulled a muscle during the Barbados–MCC game. Up to that moment my mother had never watched me play first class cricket. I don't think she liked how I used to behave, when, as a boy I was sent to the store on errands. I rarely came back in time, and if the boys were playing cricket, I would not reach back for a long while. And, of course, the money sometimes went missing. However, in this Barbados game, when I pulled the muscle she was listening on the radio and heard that I was being lifted off the field. I don't know how she got to Kensington so quickly, even though we lived less than a kilometre away. But when I got into the dressing room she was the first person I saw. She cared for me, and at the same time she did not like the idea that as a boy cricket was my number one pre-occupation. I think it left a bad taste in her mouth that I could become lost mentally in a cricket game and seemed as if that was all there was in the world.

So we held out against the English and waited until the Aussies arrived in 1955. Lindwall and Miller were back, so too was Johnston who had given us more trouble with his medium fast stuff. Richie Benaud, whom we encountered in 1951, had grown in stature as an excellent leg-spinner. We still had Ram and Val, and Gary was added to the line up which Frank King led with the new ball. Young Collie Smith had emerged as a batsman for the future. It was already being said that Sobers and Smith would be the core of the middle order after the 3Ws.

Atkinson was promoted to the captaincy after Stollmeyer, a decision that most people felt was a part of the ongoing refusal to give Frank the respect that was due to him. Nobody who knew the game's history could have justified the decision, but the WICBC made its thinking clear to all of us. In the end we were beaten convincingly by a margin of 3-0.

We lost the first Test at Sabina Park by 9 wickets. Neil Harvey and Keith Miller made solid centuries in a total of 515. We did not come up to scratch despite a century, 108 by Clyde. I was run out on 19, and Collie fought bravely for 44, but we never really recovered. Bowled out for 259, the Aussies enforced the follow on. Collie slammed a good century but the total of 275 was not enough.

As always, Queens Park Oval was the hunting ground for the 3Ws and I felt comfortable with the weight of history behind us. Stollmeyer returned as captain and Atkinson was dropped. We pressed very hard to win the second Test but had to suffice with a draw. Clyde and I got centuries, 126 and 139 respectively against the four pace attack of Miller, Lindwall, Johnston and Archer. It was Clyde's second in two matches and he looked invincible. He took on the pace with some scorching drives and pulls. It was pretty rough stuff coming down, and Clyde gave it the treatment.

The Aussies responded to our 382 with a massive 600 for 9 declared. We struggled to penetrate on the pitch, and in addition to the three centuries by batsmen C. McDonald, A. Morris and N. Harvey, bowlers Archer and Lindwall got half centuries.

In the second innings Clyde hammered another century (110), and I was left stranded at the end of the game on 87 not out. That kind of thing was becoming a habit, or so it seemed at the time. Frank did not play in this game and we missed him with both bat and ball.

Sobers played an excellent little first innings knock of 47 and was not out on 8 with me in the second innings. We had a good relationship, and this was reflected in our batting together. I saw myself as a mentor of sorts. I had given him a bat when he made his debut for Barbados, and took considerable interest in his welfare. He was coming along very nicely, and in the field he was fast becoming something very special. All of this gave me much pleasure.

Though we lost the third Test at Bourda, the pleasure of watching Gary's maturity into a Test player continued to grow. In fact, his 3 for 20 from 16 overs in Australia's second innings was perhaps the most memorable part of the disaster, from a West Indian point of view. It is true that Benaud did well, taking 4 for 15 from 3.5 overs. And it would be remiss of me not to say that he took my wicket when I had reached 81, which turned out to be the top score in our first innings. I did not trouble the scorers in the second innings and Clyde top scored with 73, but there is no doubt that our batting was failing as a unit, and the Aussies were on top of us, notwithstanding Clyde's excellent form.

There was an opportunity for the Barbadian players to get some further exposure to the Aussies in the Barbados X1 game. It had become a bit of a tradition for Barbados to give visiting Test teams a run for their money, and large crowds would assemble to witness what were sometimes more competitive matches than Test. Gary struck an aggressive 62 in the match, a signal to selectors that he had become a class batsman, even though they had seen him from the beginning as a bowler, the one who had replaced Val in the Jamaica Test against England the previous year. I felt pretty good about the 132 runs I added to the score, and hoped of course that it could be repeated in the Test.

The fourth Test at Kensington has gone down in the history books as one of the great thrillers. Responding to the Aussie first innings total of 668, including centuries from the two great fast bowlers, Lindwall (118) and Miller (137), we reached 510 with the historic partnership between Atkinson (219), who captained in place of Stollmeyer, and wicketkeeper Clairemont Depeiza (122), batting at nos. 6 and 7 respectively. The partnership of 348 was celebrated as the greatest ever played at Kensington; that two Bajans were at the wicket added to the local flavour. But it was the 43 by Gary that captured the imagination of the Oval and set the place ablaze with excitement.

Gary was sent in to open and took a turn in Miller in a way that I am sure he has never forgotten. In short time he had smacked 10 fours off the new ball with some of the most amazing shots imaginable. It was theatre at its best. I have heard many people describe this innings in many ways suggesting that it is now a story of legend and lore. Miller ended with figures of 2 for 113 from 22 overs, not his most satisfying performance. We went on the attack and soon had the Aussies all out for 249. Val, Ram and Frank took no wickets, neither did Tom Dewdney, our young pacer. It was Atkinson's royal match to which he added to his double century figures of 5 for 56 from 36 overs. There was no time to press for victory, though Clyde, our in-form batsman, raced to 83 before being bowled by Benaud.

We received the final hammering at Sabina Park in the 5th Test, losing by an inning and 82 runs. Clyde continued his excellent form hitting 155. Miller bounced back from his Barbados beating to capture 6 for 107. Then the slaughter came when the Aussies struck 758 for 8 declared, with 5 centuries, one of which was a double (Harvey 204). In our second innings, Clyde proved himself the best batsman in the world in 1955, hitting 110 while we fell to 319 all out. I was left on 36 not out, after I had gone in at no. 9.

The 3-0 defeat confirmed that the Aussies were a better side, though it seemed a mystery to some that England had twice defeated them. While Clyde confirmed his great class once he was freed of wicket keeping duties, it was being said that the middle order comprised of the 3-Ws was losing its edge. But there was more to it than this. We continued to lack a pair of genuine pacers, and Ram and Val who had done magic for us over the decade, were being blunted by a new batting technique that entailed the constant use of the trusting left pad. While Gary and Collie were looking good for the future, and we had excellent performances such as that by Atkinson in the Barbados Test, we lacked the balance possessed by Australia and England.

We fell from the lofty heights of 1950 to the deep valley of despair by the end of the tour of 1955. The statistics do not make for pleasant West Indian reading: 20 matches, 4 victories, 7 draws, and 9 defeats. I had scored quite consistently, as did Frank and Clyde but we could not halt the decline. The issue here was that we were not all performing at the same time as in earlier years which allowed opposition teams to penetrate our defenses. We were looking to brilliant individual performances to deliver the team, which was not the way we had built winning ways in earlier years. It seemed we had returned to the old days when George lifted his game only to watch the team fall.

If 1955 was a bad dream, 1957 in England was our worst nightmare. But I did go to bed with a smile on my face because I had a pretty good series the previous year against the New Zealanders. The WICBC took the decision to conduct selection experiments with the tour. It was a chance to rest some senior players, but more importantly it was an opportunity to see what we had in store with respect to the younger players. We were without the services of Rae, Stollmeyer and Gomez. Stollymeyer had hung up his boots after a long and distinguished career. Gomez was solid as a rock in the middle and was more than a useful seamer. Stollmeyer was the elder statesman, and was at the ripe old age of 34 while Gomez was 35. Stolly had played 32 Test and averaged 42 with four centuries while Gomez had played 29 Tests, averaged 30 with one century but had taken 58 wicket at 27 each.

I was asked to carry the additional responsibility with the bat, not the captaincy. Frank and Clyde were not available, but I still had my two shipmates, Ram and Val. We started out about the same time and understood the special nature of that timing for our friendship. The WICBC also made two decisions that were not surprising even though controversial. It appointed Goddard, already retired, to lead the tour as player and manager. And the captaincy was given to Denis Atkinson. Frank was once again placed in a position that was very awkward, and for many people it was another instance of the continuing victimization. At the time Frank's leadership claims were strong and obvious, but the powers that be did not see it that way.

For obvious reasons I was determined to carry the bag for Frank and Clyde, and felt it was important to do so. We were the 3Ws and that meant, as far as I was concerned that, like the three musketeers, it would be one for all and all for one. Then we had the good news of having young Gary and Collie in the middle. So we had some important changes, but we were balanced with the new boys, among whom was Dewdney, the improving pacer from Jamaica.

We won the first Test at Dunedin by an innings and 71 runs. Ram and Val ran through the hosts without much resistance; Ram was back in action with 6 for 23 from 21 overs. They were all out for 74. I remember that 5 persons didn't score and that the top score was 23. When it was our turn to bat Gary was going beautifully before he was run out on 27. He was sent in at three, testament to the recognition that he was a greatly improved batsman. Collie and I stuck it out and at the end of the innings of 353 he had made 64 and I was generously given 123. We wrapped up their second innings for 208 and retired for a few days of well earned rest.

The second Test at Christ Church produced a similar result. I was allowed to score another century (103) in the first innings from a total of 386. I remember thinking how wonderful it would be to score one for both Frank and Clyde. But it could not be in the match because we bowled out our host twice, for 158 and 164. Ram took five in the first innings and Val took five in the second. We also won the third Test, this time by nine wickets. I was able to give effect to my wish of honouring Frank and Clyde with a third century, 156 in the first innings. Our hosts won the fourth and final Test by 190 runs. It was one of those strange low scoring matches in which we made 145 and 77 while our host made 255 and 157.

I scored a few other centuries in the first class matches but the 123, 103, and 156 in Tests allowed the good folks at *Wisden Cricket Magazine* to vote me the best batsman in the world in 1956. It was a welcomed return to high performance consistency. It was an important moment in my career as a Test player. I am aware that Michael Manley in his study of the series noted that I had "returned to form". Well, maybe that was the case, but to me it was more about putting injury out of my mind and getting on with the business of batting. Talk had been everywhere that I was not the same man as I was in the early 1950s.

It is a very difficult argument to combat because I do not know of anyone or anything that does not get older and feel the impact of age. What I would say is that many people knew how serious my injury had been but were of the view that a half performing Weekes was still an asset, hence the very dangerous matter of playing for long with injury. For sure my legs were not as quick, and the *Novocain* I was injecting had its toll on my reflexes. But I loved cricket, and representing the West Indies was an honour I took very, very, seriously.

In my less than perfect condition I had made six centuries in ten innings, and ended with an average of 104 in the first class matches. A few writers fussed about my number one world rating by Coopers and Lybrand. I think the rating gave me 907 points ahead of Peter May (902) and Neil Harvey (887).

Everton Weekes: Coopers and Lybrand Rating (3 March 1956)

Top Ten Batsmen	Points
1. E. de C. Weekes	907
2. P.B.H. May	902

3. R.N. Harvey........................ 887
4. C.L. Walcott....................... 884
5. D.J. McGlew........................ 839
6. D.C.S. Compton................. 824
7. C.C. McDonald.................. 766
8. L. Hutton........................... 740
9. W.R. Endean...................... 690
10. P.R. Umrigar...................... 672

The rating experts noted that the 156 I scored in the third Test against New Zealand was my third consecutive Test match century which moved my rating from 888 to its peak of 907. This they said meant that I overtook Peter May 'to become the number one rated batsman in the world'. The report ended with the comment that this was the second time I was rated 'number one in the world'. The first instance, the report stated, was in 1950 after I had scored the five consecutive centuries followed by five half centuries in the next seven Test innings. None of this impressed my banker, but I generously thanked Coopers and Lybrand for its role in enhancing popular perceptions of my status and reputation.

The 1957 tour of England was when the bottom fell out the West Indian bucket. Frank wrote at a later date that we lost the series on the boat going over to England. He made reference to the class and race factors that got in the way of team unity. Especially important was the matter of differences in the quality of accommodation. In those days you paid for what you could afford, and some of the boys could afford luxury facilities and others were stranded literally, like Jonah, in the bowels of the ship. These things cannot be ignored. While such conditions also applied to 1950, the difference was that we were not a team in 1950 until we got to England. We were assembled in England and there most of us got to know each other. This was seven years later, and we had played a lot of cricket together. Many of us had become friends, and the 3Ws, like Ram and Val, had already gained legendary dimension. The inequality in experience impacted personally, and very deeply.

England was hot for revenge. We held them to a draw in 1954 after they had defeated the Aussies twice in succession. They were in the position in which we found ourselves in 1950. If they could take us out they could declare themselves world leaders. Even though Hutton had retired while on top, May replaced him as captain and was rated by Coopers and Lybrand the second best batsman in the world. Also, it was clear he had the respect of his men, and acquired the status, in short time, as a very clever captain.

Lock and Laker, the new spin twins, were respected as a formidable pair, and were joined by the now mature and very effective pace partners, Trueman and Statham. Backing up these hunting pairs was Bailey, the old fox of English cricket who joined with Evans, the veteran, to bring maturity to the middle. May in the middle was backed by Colin Cowdrey and Tom Graveney. For sure, England in 1957 was a balanced and well oiled piece of machinery. They were on top of their game.

On the other hand, we were not as strong as we were in 1954. Our openers, Rae and Stollmeyer, were retired and we had not replaced them to good effect. Ram and Val could still do it but were overbowled and the signs of fatigue were setting in. Collie and Gary had not yet hit high speed, though they were evolving rapidly. Gomez was retired and we were blooding Roy Gilchrist and Wes Hall, both very fast and hostile but young and inexperienced. We had long decided to give Clyde a rest from the gloves, and against Australia he was universally recognized as the world's most destructive batsman. The decision was taken to give the gloves to a young and inexperienced Rohan Kanhai, also a brilliant prospect with the bat, but not fully ready for the high intensity game. The 3Ws, aged, but not old, would be in the middle.

We were off to an excellent start in the first Test at Edgbaston, until we ran into a brick wall called May and Cowdrey. If in 1950 we could sing the song, "London Bridge is falling down", I supposed it would have been appropriate now to sing "Rock of ages cleft for me". In the first innings Ram ran through the host team in a way that brought back memories of 1950. He picked up 7 for 49 from 31 overs and sent familiar shivers down the English spine. Val did not play in this game, and his place was taken by Atkinson. Ram was on fire. They could not pick him, and like the New Zealanders, they looked out of sorts attempting both defensive and attacking shots.

We responded as if we were smelling blood, and piled on a massive 474 in response to their 186. Clyde was caught behind off Laker for a big 90; Frank struck a very polished 81, and I, who was bowled by Trueman for 9, had the satisfaction of seeing Collie, tipped as my successor, smashing a memorable 161, his first century in England. Sobers was also well on his way with a well crafted 53 before Bailey, his first Test wicket caught him off Statham. From there, as the saying goes, the rest was history. In England's second innings May and Cowdrey went to work and established a match saving partnership of 411. When the innings was declared on 583 for 4, May was left on 285 not out, and Cowdrey had scored 154.

It was not just an excellent piece of art to watch; it was monumental. It has been described as the greatest partnership in the history of Test cricket. It certainly broke every record in English middle order batting, and more importantly, it broke the back of our bowling, particularly the confidence and competence of Ram, and later Val. Ram bowled 98 overs, 35 maidens, and took 2 for 179. No bowler had ever bowled so many overs in an innings in a Test match. He too established a record as the game crashed from a potential win for the Windies to an awful nightmare that left us shaken and scared. A draw might have been a fair compromise but the sheer size of the partnership was crushing to the spirit.

It was in this game that modern cricket took a turn in new directions, though I was not sure then, as I am now, if it was for the better. I was raised on batting techniques that called for the use of the bat as the primary instrument. A ball would crash into the pad when you missed it, or as a consequence of some failure of the bat. May and Cowdrey survived by developing a new approach to batting that was not before used as a standard practice. They would trust their left leg deep down the wicket to balls that were both pitched outside off, or even in line. They would attempt to play no shot, and the ball would crash into the pad. Umpires were defied. The batsman, the rules say, is to get the benefit of the doubt. But the umpire was challenged to decide whether a ball, striking the pad fully stretched down the wicket, could with any certainty strike the stumps.

During the tour, umpires decided that they could not be sure, and the batsmen were given the luxury. This meant that it was no longer necessary to play at Ram and Val unless you got to the pitch. There was no need to cut, or to get back to a ball short of a good length. It became a war of pad against Ram and Val, and aided by the umpires. They were stopped in the trenches and killed off. It was a sad and inglorious end to the two giants of the game. They were defeated not by the cunning of batsmen, but by a new methodology that spoke to survival rather than skill, cunning rather than craft. It was a strategic response from England, but the world did not consider it an improvement upon the game. I once heard it described as defending the Empire by all means necessary.

In the summer of 1957 we all contracted various degrees of laryngitis. We cried out in vain to umpires for decisions against batsmen that in previous tours would have sent them back to the dressing room. Our pleas fell on deaf ears and smiling faces; umpires merely said, 'sorry lads, not sure about that one.' It was a very depressing time. I watched Ram especially, as his spirit sunk into despair. Never before had I seen a pad used in this way. It was already ingrained in my skull that the sole purpose of the pad is to protect the shin. Now I saw it being used in place of the bat, to confront the ball. I believe that only one English wicket in five matches was given lbw to Ram, Loader, the number 11, in the very last Test. Our pacers and seamers got three lbw decisions, but Ram and Val were treated like aliens on planet earth. On the other hand 9 lbw decisions went against us.

England won the second Test at Lords by an innings and 36 runs. We were scuttled out for 127 and 261, as against the host's 424. In the second innings I managed to hold on for 90, scored mostly with Gary who batted brilliantly for 66. I have heard the pundits say it was one of my best innings, the kind of statement that only pundits could make because I was holding on for life in a dying situation. Manley has said that it is remembered 'with awe for all that it fell short of the classic milestone'. That is the kind of thing Manley would say, being a poetic politician who won elections by large margins. Bailey's eleven wickets in the match had its effect on morale. Like Bedser, he got the ball to swing in the air, and seam off the wicket. He really was a handful during the series.

We held on to a draw in the third Test at Trent Bridge, thanks to a remarkable innings by Frank who opened and came not out on 191 in the first innings and Collie's second century (168) in the second innings. Ram and Val bowled 61 overs between them in the first innings and did not take a wicket. That too was a record of some distinction. I did not do very well, scoring 33 and 3. While I do not wish to offer excuses for failure the pain and discomfort from my sinus problem were getting the upper hand. Clyde had also developed a thigh injury in the first Test that was not getting any better. The officials knew of our handicap but little was said to fans, some of whom could hear and see that all was not well. The Headingly Test saw us falling deeper into the quicksand. In the past we relied on Ram and Val to pull us out. Val was out and again Ram bowled a long spell(19 overs) that went unrewarded.

I got a king pair at the Oval which like the previous fourth Test we lost by an innings. We were wiped out for 89 and 86 against England's first innings total of 412. If ever there was a Test series massacre this was it. Our skipper Goddard did not play in the last Test, and had scored 24 and 0 not out, 1 and 21, 0 and 61, and 1 and 4 in the first four respectively. Sobers showed all of his class, top scoring in both innings of the last Test with 39 and 42. Frank was not with us in New Zealand, and had not played Test cricket for a while but was able to top the first class batting averages at 58.8 with 1,470 runs. It seemed like the end of Ram and Val as a Test force, as tragic an ending as one could imagine. They had taken some 297 Test wickets between them. Ram, nonetheless, topped the first class bowling averages with 119 on tour at the near impossible 13.8.

When it was all over, the recrimination started and there was a lot of it. Every official and fan was looking for an explanation for this disastrous failure, and the despair and disillusionment that seemed to follow. The 3Ws took their fair share of the criticism, some of it as violent as it was inaccurate. Most of it centred on the selection of Goddard as captain, and by implication the marginalization of Frank. The Goddard, Atkinson, Alexander supremacy over Frank was not cricket related. Manley, the supreme diplomat, said it was a part of a dishonourable colonial system rooted in the WICBC that was making fools and victims of honourable men.

Goddard was an honourable man, and the decision to bring him out of retirement to lead the team was not based on nostalgia alone; it was the dishonourable system setting up an honourable man to do a dishonourable thing. For sure, the racial politics was strangling West Indies cricket and threatening our achievements. To be led by Gerry Alexander in the fifth Test at Kensington Oval was not the best way to play West Indies cricket, given that his inexperience at the Test level was so glaring. He had not paid his dues, and appeared a novice in the company of Frank. But he was a nice chap, another example of the dishonourable system making a mockery of the reputations of good men.

It was the end of an era in other regards. Everything hit the fan in 1957. The public became frustrated with the race and class biases and demanded merit and democracy. It was an end of the road for some players as well as the colonial system in which I entered in 1948. West Indies began to look very closely at itself and some hard answers were emerging from the public.

The WICBC had no intention of reforming itself, but the entry of the democracy movement came over the top and toppled the backwardness. By the time we got home C.L.R. James was on the campaign trail demanding Frank as captain while the WICBC had already indicated that Alexander was the chosen one.

We had four months to prepare for the Pakistan visit. I was concerned about my health as Clyde was bothered about his injury. There were rumors of multiple retirements. We were all worried about Frank. He was taking an emotional beating that was unfair and vicious, and there was little we could do about it. The WICBC was in the of hands the Trinidadian grandee, Sir Errol Dos Santos, with whom few persons were prepared to cross swords. Through him, the members of the Board called the shots, and players were without the kind of power they have today. The public was determined to break his power in terms of the selection of the captaincy, and only a man with the stature and reach of James could have effectively launched and won the struggle. Frank was not available to play in the Pakistan series under the captaincy of Alexander, the Jamaican Cambridge University graduate in veterinary medicine.

We had some early revenge in the first Test in Barbados. The game took more or less the same turn as the first Test against England at Edgbaston. This was a very disturbing sign for us because it suggests that we were now a team that could win early credit but lacked the power to finish the job. We rattled up 579 in the first innings. Conrad Hunte, setting out on his glorious but short career, smashed 142. Gary came in at no. 3 and gave us a polished 52. Collie, now so very reliable, scored 78 and Clyde 43. Nature smiled on me one more time and I was able to add 197 to the total. Of course I was frustrated by this tendency to get out in the '90, even though I was told many years before never to play flashy cuts in the '90s. Pakistan was reduced to 106, thanks mainly to an excellent spell of pace by Roy Gilchrist who took two early wickets and came back to wrap up the tail.

But we could not finish the work. As was the case in the first Test in England the opposition's second innings spelled disaster for us. This was the match in which the legendary Hanif Mohammad scored the monumental 337, landing Pakistan with a total of 657 for 8 declared. Ram was virtually, but not officially, retired but Val, soldiering on, bowled 39 overs and took 2 for 109, not the kind of return he was accustomed to experiencing. His two wickets were not those of recognized batsmen, and he was dropped after this game, a tearful farewell for a great superstar at the age of 30.

We won the second Test at Queen's Park Oval in a closely fought battle. The middle order performed well, though without any centuries. Gary, now in stride, scored 52 and 80, and I was able to chip in with 78 run out and 24. Kanhai was like a bright spark, and his 96 in the second innings showed his artistry. By the time we arrived in Jamaica, it was clear that the lads were feeling something that reminded me of the good old days of the early 1950s. We could feel that Hunte was made of something special and that he had extraordinary powers of concentration that reminded me of my youth. Maybe it was his BCL training that gave him an inward hunger for runs. He tortured the bowling in that magnificent innings of 260 run out that has unfairly been over-shadowed by the enormity of the superlative record breaking 365 not out by the emerged Gary.

For some of us it was like watching a train approaching. Gary was showing all the necessary abilities needed for greatness, even though he fell far too often just short of a century. Sabina Park was all party. Gary was very stylist and the fans loved his flair and theatrical glory. Carnival broke out and we watched the greatest of West Indies cricket being celebrated by the people not yet independent. And Gary did not end there. We won the fourth Test at Bourda comfortably on account of Gary's 125 and 109 not out, in the first and second innings respectively, opening the batting in place of Kanhai who moved down to no. 6. Clyde's 145 in the first innings was a clear sign that he was still on top of his game and had recovered sufficiently from his thigh injury. Pakistan bounced back to win the fifth Test in Trinidad, but we had already won the series with a 2 win lead.

This was the end of the road for me as a Test player. I announced my retirement and called it a day after ten years in the middle. I was 33 years old, but was feeling a little older on the inside. There was immediate speculation about my decision. Was I pulled into retirement by an aging mind-body relationship, or was I pushed by management? Well, there had been hints and the occasional accusation in high places that we lost the 1957 series against England because the 3Ws would not invest time and energy in getting into match fitness condition. Remarks of this kind were made by Cecil DeCaires, a senior official in 1957. He made general comments about my fitness, and implied that I was not doing enough to get prepared for Test assignments.

I was advised to seek legal counsel. After all, I was a professional cricketer. Word got to Sir Errol of my intention to litigate and he suggested to me that having lost the series we shouldn't take the business of West Indies Cricket into the streets. The idea of seeking legal counsel came from a gentleman named Errol Barrow. He was insisting that I take the Board to court for suggesting that I should step down when playing cricket was my livelihood and the selectors were happy with my presence. Errol set up a legal group across the Caribbean, including Hugh Wooding from Trinidad, and the Premier of British Guiana, Forbes Burnham. Sir Errol was asked to issue a statement on behalf of the WICBC, and he did.

There the matter ended.

TEN

SOME REFLECTIONS ON
TODAY'S PLAYERS

FIRST, I WILL COMMENT on the common practice of players hugging and kissing when a wicket falls. It is a good thing to see such celebrations. Frank did not believe in it. He felt it gave people the impression we were not accustomed to success. It would not have gone down very well in my time, in any event. Goodness, can you imagine me rushing up to Goddard and hugging him like a brother? And can you really envisage Frank, Clyde or I dashing up to Stollmeyer and planting an embrace around his neck?

I have had over 40 years to reflect on how the game has evolved at the level of the player as well as the administrator. The first idea that comes to your mind in terms of how my generation went about its business, and what seemed to have changed in the current game, is the role of values and philosophy. I am aware that aspects of society have to change, and that each generation sees the world differently. But while we must embrace change, we have to be careful not to throw out the baby with the bath water.

It comes down to a few words, big words, I must admit, but simple in meaning; determination, commitment, and love. I was driven by these concepts, and set out on a quest to master the art of batting. I wanted to know all about it. Every aspect of it fascinated me and I wanted to learn the rules, embrace the principles, and perfect the methods. Also, I wanted to know why it was that I wanted to do these things. I discovered that the reason extended beyond my pocket, or my village. It had to do with being told that because I was poor and without a higher education I had no intellect with which to work. I was born and raised in a community that loved cricket, and therefore I wanted to master the thing that the village considered important to its well being.

Most things, including the journey to excellence, begin with the individual. Then you move from self to community, and to country, and each time you see how important it is to master what you are doing. Then you see the international picture, because all Test cricketers are members of a family. I wanted respect within the family, and I had to earn it. For me, the core was commitment and determination.

Mastery requires the application of commonsense and a measure of science. For example, you have to apply your intelligence to the things that are commonly known in order to find the level of dedication needed. One of the key issues, for example, is learning how to practice sensibly. I have seen many young chaps over the years, as well as some experienced players, just whacking the ball around the ground and all over the place in practice sessions. My preference was to get a bowler to bowl at my weaknesses in order to improve technique and concentration. Too many players today are not prepared to admit that they have weaknesses. This suggests that intelligence is not being applied because all players have weaknesses and they can be turned into strengths only after they are recognized.

I suspect that pride has something to do with it, but it would have to be false pride if a chap does not wish to learn as a result of self-criticism. I was aware of the movement of my feet and hands. If I recognized that there was a problem I was the first who wanted to know because my objective is not pride but scoring runs.

The only pride a batsman should have is the kind that speaks to scoring runs and playing for his country. I cannot speak enough about practicing sensibly, because when I was playing at the Club level I would try to make sure that I practiced sensibly. Today there are machines that can be programmed to work as you wish, and this is an important support tool. But the batsman must be prepared to accept that there is an aspect of his method and technique than can be improved, but the journey begins with self-acknowledgment.

The process of removing weaknesses begins with assessing accurately how you are getting out, or where you are not scoring runs. We have a good case in point here with one member of the current West Indies team − Dwayne Smith who gets out too often playing the same sort of stroke. To a lesser extent, a couple of years earlier, the present Vice-Captain of the West Indies, Sarwan, would get out playing the sort of stroke that quicker bowlers recognized was his weakness. They would bowl him a couple of half-volleys to bring him onto the front foot and then the short-pitched delivery. By then he had made 20 or so. But he is a much better player than 20. It looked as though at one stage he might have been able to erase that weakness, but since the mental rigour has not gone into the weakness eradication it continues to lurk to his downfall.

Steve Waugh absolutely refused at a moment in his career to play a hook shot. The result was that he got a lot of runs by surviving and turning the tables on the bowlers. He frustrated our bowlers because he refused to fall to their game plan. He decided how he would bat, and where he would score. It was a smart mental adjustment that many young players should consider. Bowlers can be defeated when a batsman calls the shots out in the middle. When you say to a good bowler, I have no weakness you can exploit, it reduces him to ordinariness.

Frank also stopped playing the hook shot. He realized from very early that by hitting the ball behind square leg, he had more control over where the ball would go. So he got inside the line and smashed it backward. To hit the ball in front of square leg you have to be in possession of many skills, not one or two. You have to be honest enough and smart enough to know if you have all the skills of height, eyes, arms, legs, shoulders, and reflexes, to hit the ball safely forward of square. Honesty with self is therefore a key component, and too many young players today do not have this conversation with themselves. There is too much denial, and you cannot be a great player unless you are true to yourself.

The deep source of the problem with young Smith is that he plays too many balls across the line, hitting to mid-wicket when he should be driving the ball straight. The problem is that he does not score many runs on the off-side and therefore goes into the on-side seeking compensation. He goes looking for the water rather than allow the water to come to him. He doesn't seem to have enough off-side shots, and as a result he has created a leg side problem. What he needs to do, in my judgment, is to forget the leg side problem and practice a wider range of off-side and down the wicket shots.

I have seen Smith play some long innings and I know he can play all those strokes – the cover drive and the square cut. He is potentially a very good player but he needs help with the mind game. There is need for him to understand that mastery takes time and care and considerable mental application. A batsman's intellect is his best friend. He is on his way to high performance consistency when he realizes that the mind delivers the shots, not the arms.

The same mental skill that makes Smith an excellent fielder is what he should use when batting. Most great batsmen are excellent fielders. Neil Harvey was the greatest all-round fieldsman I saw, even though great men like Colin Bland, Clive Lloyd and Viv Richards were only a whisper behind. Being an excellent fielder is more than just being quick in the field. Many chaps today cover the ground very quickly but do not gather and throw with precision.

The mental power aspect is vital. It is the easiest thing in the world for a batsman to develop anxiety, which breeds nervousness. These two states of mind are the killers of batsmen. The first lesson of the batting craft is to fight anxiety and push back nervousness. I have seen in the eyes of some batsmen the anxiety of race horses; you cannot make a hundred with a few hurried strokes. Scoring a century is like building a house; you have to put in the foundation and build up the walls and put in the windows and doors.

Runs come in different shapes and forms and they all add to the beauty of the structure. A house with only big doors will not work because small windows allow the big door to have definition and a wider sense of purpose. Lara has proven this point time and time again. All of his great innings were well crafted and designed. Gary began to get the big ones when he discovered self-control and tightened his defense. At that stage his shots really became magical. That straight bat defense Gary showed the bowlers broke their hearts as much as the shot that sent the ball sizzling pass their legs.

This is my biggest concern today; too many of the younger players are not trying hard enough to understand the mind aspect of the game, and this is why more of the players of earlier times were more consistent. Recently, I was listening to a radio programme and someone called in to suggest that we have so many tall young men around the region, and that we should take some of them and enroll them into a school for fast bowlers. Now this is fine up to a point. But there is more to it. Fast bowling has a high mental endurance factor, that is where the grit and stamina, determination and strength come in. In addition you have to add love for the craft and an appreciation of the science.

Being tall and strong is important but it is not enough to produce a good fast bowler. We have had some excellent pacers, and all of them have been pretty sharp upstairs. The ones that fell by the wayside, and they were many, fell as a result of either injury or ignorance. Ian Bishop was on his way to greatness and fell to injury, but there was a large number that refused to become thinkers. These had very short careers.

Malcolm Marshall and Michael Holding, for example, were very smart young men who had superb heads on their shoulders, as did Wes Hall, Andy Roberts, Curtly Ambrose and Courtney Walsh, and all the others who made us proud over the years. For most of the time I played Test cricket we relied on spinners and seamers. We had a number of good pacers but they were not as reliable and consistent as the spinners and seamers. We have tended to under-estimate what an excellent seamer Frank was. But he did very well for us, and so did Gerry Gomez and Denis Atkinson.

It is difficult to imagine spinners who were as destructive over a decade in the way that Ram and Val ripped everyone apart. Shane Warne is obviously a class player, one of the very best. It would be interesting to compare his impact on Australian success with Ram and Val on West Indies success. Richie Benaud was a very smart cricketer, very much a thinker in the way that Malcolm Marshall and Imran Khan were clever in terms of being able to read a game.

Despite the enormous impact of Ram and Val we have been more prolific in producing pacers. Real pacers are hard to come by; the chaps who could hit 90 miles and stay there for a while with length and line. Charles Griffith and Wes Hall were quick, and very dangerous. If they got any assistance from the pitch you needed help from above to cope with them. Wes was faster than Charlie Griffith, but when Charlie was motivated, if someone upset him for example, then I am not sure because he could step up the pace and precision by several notches.

On the English side, Trueman was as quick as anyone today, but Frank Tyson was the fastest thing that I have seen, including all of the above. Tyson was particularly dangerous with the body line attack, and he moved the ball a lot through the air as Marshall did. Holding and Marshall on their day were excellent models that other fast bowlers should try to emulate. The control with pace and swing is a gift and they had more than their fair share of it. But having a gift is only 80% of the business of success. These two men worked hard at their game, did a lot of thinking and analysis, and mastered the mind game in the way that my generation went about it.

As West Indians we started out our Test journey in the late twenties, with what we now call a four prong pace attack – Learie Constantine, Herman Griffith, George Francis, and Manny Martindale. It was a battery of pace for sure, but it did not bring us the results. We were up against some very great batsmen at the time. The Australians had Ponsford and Bradman, truly great batsmen. The English had Herbert Sutcliffe, Jack Hobbs and Wally Hammond. These guys could get runs against any attack, and they piled them up against our pacers. And they made some pretty big scores at that.

At a later date the English produced Dennis Compton, Peter May, and Len Hutton, all class players with an appetite for big scores. I am not sure England has produced batsmen of this calibre in recent years, though Ian Botham was a very fine player who would be an asset to any team.

In terms of durability, it should be said that players of my time did not play half as many matches as they do today. Gary was the great exception. Consider that Stollmeyer played 32 Tests, Rae 15, Clyde 44, Gomez 29, Ram 43 and Val 36. I played 48 Tests in the ten years and today if you can maintain your place over ten years you are going to play 100 Tests. The pacers are the ones who are suffering the most in the current game. In the case of the West Indies, our current crop is very young but also comparatively small men. Some of them are as quick as those who went before but their productivity is low, but this has a lot to do with mental shortcomings.

Our batsmen are also small chaps, in a sense they are within my tradition. Gayle, is the biggest man on the side, and he shows the power of his size, as did Clyde. Greenidge and Haynes were strong, tough looking fellows. George Headley and I were two of the smallest men who played for the West Indies, and I believe that Lara fits comfortably into this company. Not much ahead were chaps like Lawrence Rowe and Rohan Kanhai.

But of course the game is played in the head and physical size is not a critical variable for either bowlers or batsmen. Marshall and Gilchrist were both small men and were probably the fastest we have had. But, it all happens between the ears. You have to live and sleep the game in order to get into its logic. After you have got there and you understand, then you can back off and relax a little. But you must climb up as if you are mounting a horse. You cannot do like the ladies and train the horse to stoop down so you can mount. You have to climb up there, and each time you fall, get back until you succeed, and begin to look the part.

I had a very strange experience in England in 1950. We were playing in a county game. I was a 190 overnight – the game in which I got the 100 in 65 minutes and then took 40 minutes to get 10. But that night I just about managed to stop myself from falling off the bed because I was running the single to reach 200. This is a true story. I woke up just in time. After the game was finished I did not try to let it go, as is the norm today. I would go through it, stage by stage, time and time again, until I was satisfied I understood why it went the way it did.

One of the criticisms leveled against the current West Indies players is that they don't seem to take on deeply, emotionally, their failures. Some say they move to leisure too quickly after losing games, and not enough time is given to reflection and self-criticism. If this is true then they are clearly not engaging in the learning process which is a must for professionals. Every ball that got me out was the subject of much thought. I wanted to know how on earth that could have happened and I really wanted to know why. After a while I give the bowler credit, but I wanted to know why and how I contributed to his celebration. Each time a chap celebrated my wicket I felt as if I was the one who bought the drinks for someone's party to which I was not invited. And that kind of feeling used to hurt a little bit.

Then there is the physical aspect, which in my opinion, speaks to a kind of mental withdrawal. For instance, I am not impressed with the idea of players arriving at the post game programme dressed in vests and slippers. It looks a little too flimsy and suggests that no rigorous thinking is taking place. Some say that it is sloppy, and I share this view because I do believe there is a strong connection between the mind and general social conduct.

It has been said that the financial security of contemporary players has a lot to do with this state of mind. But a person who is guaranteed a large income should be very concerned about high performance levels and images. Such a person should be investing in being able to produce more each year, and looking the part. I would wish to link my wage bargaining to my performance, and at the end of the day feel that justice was served. Showing up to play without the mental machinery and the psychological profile all lined up and ready to go is really not a fair exchange for a competitive salary.

The real challenge in all of this is whether the skill level and the stature of the game have fallen while the entertainment level has increased along with incomes. I think not. There is still considerable skill within the game, not only in West Indies cricket, but everywhere, especially in South Africa, England and Australia. These are the teams that I have seen a lot of. But India is mass producing some very talented players, and it is hard to imagine it getting better than Dravid and Tendulkar.

I know it is often said, for example, that our young West Indian pacers do not have adequate ball management skills, and cannot therefore get the ball to do what they would wish. Marshall, when he was head coach, was concerned about this and charged that too many of them did not know the theoretical basics, how to in-swing and out-swing, and so on. Some of this is true, because there are many boys playing at first class level who lack the technical knowledge that is needed to produce the skill. Not enough cricket is played at the highest level, and it is possible to find players who are seriously knowledge deficient.

When you consider, for instance, that my generation knew all of the technical aspects of the game as teenagers, and went to the first class level in order to implement what we knew, and to learn some new tricks from oldsters, it is hard to imagine players learning the basics on the job at the Test level. But this is now a reality in the West Indies, and it is a very bad sign indeed.

Fidel Edwards seems to be losing his ability to swing the ball as his pace increases. Clearly, this is something that has to be watched and managed. More often than not it is the movement that gets a batsman undone. In my time Bedser and Bailey made the ball wobble at 75 miles an hour, and picked up a lot of wickets. Frank was excellent at this, and oftentimes got more wickets per match than the opening bowler who was twenty miles an hour faster. Walsh picked up the bulk of his wickets bowling in the 70–78 miles per hour range, and this is why

Glen McGrath is at the top of the fast bowlers' mountain.

But with technical competence and mental strength, a batsman could overcome all of this and score a lot of runs, as we did against Bedser and Bailey. Even the pacers in the 90 miles lane got their fair share of stick from us because we focused on technical correctness and mental preparation. Lindwall and Miller had express pace, and I believe we racked up many centuries against them even though they made inroads into our line-up, and in the end defeated us. One or two of us struggle against them, but certainly the 3Ws met them and did what we had to do.

Clyde was the most prolific batsman in the world in 1957, and did not spare the Aussie pace attack. It really was something to see; very much like Viv in the 1980s and Lara in the 1990's. Gary, of course, had worked very hard to remove any weakness in his batting and played real pace with as much ease as excellent spin. But the thing about Gary, as with all great players, was his mental application, discipline, and patience. He knew that sooner or later you were going to come into his comfort zone, and he was like a cat. When you made a bad move he just jumped all over you.

I have observed with some modern players, that style appears to be more important than technique. This is unfortunate. Headley and I were described as unorthodox, but we got the work done without being accused of being inelegant. Frank, Gary and Lawrence Rowe were naturally graceful, as was David Gower of England and Gregg Chappell of Australia. This was something that was a natural part of the make up of these players. When Hooper, for example, got his head down and grafted, he scored more runs and seemed more mature in his approach. The flashy twenties and thirties for which he became

181

notorious did not reflect his true potential. He had all the technical attributes to be a great player, but lacked the mental program. More often than not he gave it away. He had the gift of God in his beauty as well as the weakness of man.

A principal negative comment made about the younger West Indian players is that they are not motivated by something bigger than themselves; whether it is playing for their country, for nationalist pride, or the dignity of the Caribbean on the world stage. If you play for something that is larger than yourself you are likely to reach the highest standards. If you are not motivated by these kinds of social and political issues you are likely to fall short at precisely the moments when digging into the psychic reserves is necessary. Some people can motivate themselves by the promise of great sums of money, and others need a philosophy to guide their highest actions. Some batsmen are motivated by the basic pride involved in saying 'this bowler cannot get me out'.

It is generally believed that there is a debilitating tension between the younger and older players within the West Indies fraternity, and that this is based on the massive gaps that exist between salaries then and now. I am sure that Lara makes more in a year than Sobers made in ten, but they are very close friends. I have seen it this way: life is a relay race, and someone has to run the last leg. The one who runs the last leg gets more media attention and public celebration even though it is a relay and all legs are equally important. The generation before mine did the heavy lifting. We in turn did our share, and gave the younger chaps a better pitch on which to bat.

Sobers gave us world champion status for the first time. Remember that under Sobers we defeated Australia 2-1 in 1964/5, England 3-1 in 1966, and India 2-0 in 1966/7. This achievement is often overlooked but it was precisely what we tried to do in 1951 in Australia. Sobers did it, and gave us the first taste of elite status. The Lloyd-Richards generation really did us proud in the mid-1970s and 1980s. After we fell in 1968, losing to England, it was a decade before they picked us up and restored our leadership position. But they were able to sustain it for some fifteen years, a most remarkable achievement. In the process, they built what was clearly the strongest Test team in the history of the game.

We are now getting ready to take seriously the administration of the game. It is not an easy matter because we are supposed to be the poorest cricketing nation in the world. I have often heard it said that we have the richest legacy and the poorest economy. Even when we look at some of the recent Test playing nations, Zimbabwe and Bangladesh, it is still fair to say that in terms of wealth the West Indies remains the poorest country in the international game. This is a highly peculiar situation.

Given the lack of material resources it would be fair to say that the current state of West Indian cricket is what it should have always been. And therefore what happened in my time and after was an aberration. But it was not. It showed what can be achieved when a small community shows commitment, dedication, and discipline. We played cricket not only for the love of it, but because we loved it and therefore played it the right way for the right reasons. We need to put these factors back into the equation of play. To my judgment the future is about educational stimulation and focused training.

We did very well in the past, and this has served to produce a management system and related attitudes that have negated the importance of education and training for young cricketers. Programs have been random and ad hoc. It is not enough to

183

have a two week camp before a tour. The long term breeding of a Test player must start from the primary school system. That is when you develop a love for method and technique, and get the right attitudes with a deep thirst for runs.

We have never really had good sponsorships with investments in players until we began to lose our edge in the 1990s. This is ironic because the funds were not there when we were winning. Maybe it was thought that if you are poor and still winning, money would make you lose. I know that some people thought we were motivated to excellence because we were poor. This is not true. Poverty was painful. We were motivated by some very powerful philosophies. As a people we were trying to free ourselves from colonial bondage and cricket was a very important part of that process. We knew it, felt it, and went about our task in search of pride and honour.

The Australians were in the same position with the English, as well as the Indians. But our case was deepest because we were emerging from the legacies of slavery and economic abandonment that the Indians and Aussies never experienced. There was a strong sense of despair and struggle for justice in the Caribbean, and this embraced most of our players, black, white, Indians, and all the mixtures we had within our teams.

The players now have an organization, West Indies Players Association (WIPA) that is looking out for their welfare. It is doing so in a way that suggests the WICB might not be seeing players' welfare as its principal consideration. Relations are always tense. There is deep distrust. This is all very unfortunate, because it tells you that they are not seeing the ball clearly. The aggression shown by each CEO of WIPA sometimes frightens some people. But society will soon realize that proper representation is dealt with in the fashion of the Trade Union.

184

No one is willing to say that the WICB has its act together in a professional way. But they know that it must take responsibility for the overall state of affairs in West Indies cricket because it is charged with this duty, and this is what we all expect from it. It is a good thing for the players to have this sort of voice. It has to be a good thing for West Indies cricket.

It is time that we put some solid funds into West Indies cricket. But our success will be as a result of a combination of things. The actual knowledge preparation of the players for a tournament is vital. A series of well designed camps for practical training and educational stimulation for two to three weeks more than once a year is vital. And they must be in a facility with all the necessary support, an academy set up, so to speak.

The programmes must be enjoyable; hard work yes, but not an army camp. The boys must feel at the end of the experience that their minds have been expanded, not just their muscles. They must feel stronger on the inside. Physical training and fitness is just not enough. The mental process is about knowing why it is important to see excellence as a good and desirable thing. And they must understand the steps and processes that are required in order to get there.

I am optimistic about the future – the next ten years! I feel that we have some good players in the Caribbean who can go on for another five years with the right sort of training and education. The bowling seems to be the main challenge at the moment, but each department has its challenges. The batting is oftentimes fragile. It makes you wonder why a team like this struggles to 200 runs. They are better than that. At least they are a 270 runs team. They have four batsmen who should be able to produce a minimum team total of 250 runs on a regular basis.

There are so many role models the younger players have to draw upon, mentalities that will help them to build their mind game. The legacy is very good, but only through education will they be able to know it and use it to advantage. We must end this crisis of cricket education that is the core of our problem. Two types of mentalities are there, alive and well, for them to attach themselves. Viv had no fear. Every player should have the confidence born of a lack of fear. Gary worked very hard to remove all flaws, and he was complete, as perfect as is possible.

1928 West Indies in England. The First Ever Awarded Test Status
Standing: M.P. Fernandes, C.R. Browne, W. St. Hill, E.A. Rae, J. Neblett,
E.L.G. Hoad, J.A. Small, F.R. Martin, L.N. Constantine, C.A. Roach.
Sitting: G.N. Francis, C.V. Wight (Vice Captain), E.L. Bartlett, R.K. Nunes
(Captain), H.C. Griffith, G. Challenor, J. Scheult (Asst. Manager), O.C. Scott

1939 West Indies in England
Standing: W. Ferguson (Scorer), Gerry Gomez, J.B. Stollmeyer, L.G. Hylton,
Tyrell Johnson, C.B. Clarke, Peter Bailey, A.V. Williams
Sitting: George Headley, Ivan Barrow, R.S. Grant (Captain), J.M. Kidney
(Manager), J.H. Cameron, L.N. Constantine, E.A. Martindale
Front Row: K.H. Weekes, J.E.D. Sealey, V.H. Stollmeyer

Bacup cricket club, Lancashire, 1951

Bacup, 1954

Everton with the Hon. Freddie Miller, leader of the Barbados Labour
Party, 1966

Everton with Valentine, Pierre, and Trestrail circa. 1948

First Test, 1954 West Indies team vs England at Sabina Park
Standing: M. Fredricks, J.K. Holt (Jnr.), E.S. Kentish, A.L. Valentine, C.A. McWatt,
B. Paraideau, S. Ramadhin.
Sitting: E.D. Weekes, G.E. Gomez, J.B. Stollmeyer (Captain), G.A. Headley, C.L. Walcott.

The West Indies tour party which gave us the first Test series victory in England, 1950
W. Ferguson (Scorer), A.L. Valentine, C.L. Walcott, H.H. Johnson, L.R. Pierre,
A.F. Rae, R. Marshall, C.B. Williams.
Front Row – E. Weekes, R.J. Christiani, J.B. Stollmeyer, J.D. Goddard,
J. Kidney (Manager), G.E. Gomez, P.E. Jones, F.M. Worrell, S. Ramadhin, K.B. Trestrail

Mr. & Mrs. Weekes being presented to Her Royal Highness, Princess
Alice 18 Feb 1960

Weekes, Manager Barbados team, 1967

Weekes, first tenured black Captain of Barbados, 1960

Weekes, Manager West Indies team, 1968

Sir Everton Weekes and Barbadian Governor General, Sir Clifford Husbands

Kanhai, Headley, and Weekes, circa 1980

Meeting Princess Alice as Manager of WI team, 1968

1984, Weekes at
Kensington Oval

Sir Everton knighted, 1995

The majestic Len Hutton essays a cover drive during his twelfth Test century at
The Oval against the West Indies in the Fourth Test. Gomez, Walcott and Weekes
watched with admiration.

The famous triumvirate known as the 'Three W's' – the late Sir Frank Worrell,
the late Clyde Leopold Walcott and Sir Everton DeCourcey Weekes.

After the heroics of Ramadhin and, Valentine had made victory certain, Worrell struck to trap Johnny Wardle leg-before and end the match

Everton Weekes

Everton Weekes is bowled by a ball from Alec Bedser that would have bowled almost any batsman in the world. Weekes described Bedser as "one of the best bowlers I have ever faced".

Learie Constantine

S. Ramadhin   A.L. Valentine

Trent Bridge 1950, Everton (129) and Frank (261)

Colin Cowdrey (left) hit 154 and Peter May 285 not out in their record 4th wicket stand of 411 against West Indies, Edgbaston, 1957 tour.

Edrich is caught by Walcott off a Ramadhin leg-break. An ecstatic Prior Jones is at slip.

Sonny Ramadhin's ability to disguise his leg-cutter caused consternation for England's batsmen

Cyril Washbrook hits out at Sonny Ramadhin during England's second innings at Lord's when he scored a fighting innings of 114.

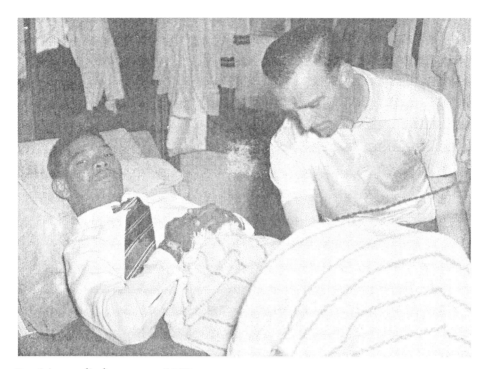

Receiving medical treatment, 1950

Everton Weekes, 1958

Sonny Ramadhin & Alf Valentine

Weekes circa 1990

Sir Everton Weekes and Sir Clyde Walcott, 2000

Sir Everton Weekes, circa 2001

With the Compliments of

THE WEST INDIES CRICKET TEAM IN GREAT BRITAIN 1950

CAPTAIN

MANAGER.

An autograph team sheet of the 1950 West Indies cricket team. It was customary for the manager of visiting teams to organise the signing of a limited number of these sheets and distribute them, upon request, to autograph collectors. Many contemporary collectors long for the return of such a custom.

THEY NOW CALL HIM
MR. BARBADOS

For the glorious victory he fashioned over MCC,
Everton Weekes gets bouquets.
By C.A. Jack Anderson

MARCH 31, 1958, was a sad one for West Indies cricket, if in the mixed feelings of most harried bowlers of other Test countries it was a happy one. It saw the start of the breaking up of the legendary Three W's – Everton Weekes and Clyde Walcott deciding to hang up their bats as far as Test cricket was concerned. In England, a studious Frank Worrell, eldest of the trio, had not decided to take that drastic step, yet he was unable to take part in the series against Pakistan, which bade farewell to his two other "musketeer" comrades, and also accept the invitation to tour India-Pakistan in 1958-59.

The Barbadian section of the current MCC tour, however, gave the opportunity to two of them to revive the lore of the W's. Weekes, becoming the first coloured cricketer to captain Barbados at home, beat Peter May's strong side by ten wickets to make Barbados the first colony to beat an MCC team in thirty years and the first time "Bimshire" themselves had enjoyed that distinction since 1926.

187

In the Test match that followed the Barbadian victory at famed Kensington Oval, Worrell was almost singularly instrumental in West Indies' fight back from 102 to 3 to pass England's 482. Worrell was able to restrain his younger but great partner at the other end, Garfield Sobers, from taking undue risks. Worrell's 197 not out will always be regarded as a monumental tribute to the skill and technique of a great player of any age because of the physical and trying conditions under which it was played and the controversy, if most from the camp of this opponents, in which it ended will long be a memory before the value of the innings will ever be forgotten.

But this is the story of Weekes, even if it is now a well-worn and known one. His inspired leadership revealed that Everton Weekes was not merely a cricketer who could and had only made runs in the best company of his time but is a cricketer who knows his cricket, as will be borne out in the account of that "famous victory" to be found elsewhere in this issue. With him as Government's Coach, Barbadian cricket should flourish among the best for many years to come.

The match provided him with the second opportunity of playing first-class cricket since his Test retirement, as he represented Barbados against British Guiana at Kensington earlier last year. His only coloured Barbadian predecessor as a captain was Herman Griffith, who was on hand to see the "victory", but the former famous West Indian fast bowler of the great trio of Learie Constantine, George Francis and Griffith, enjoyed that honour away from home when in 1941 he led Barbados in the first of the War Goodwill Series tournament at Port of Spain.

EVERTON deCOURCY WEEKES was born at Bridgetown on February 26, 1925, the second youngest and the "pocket-sized" batsman of the W's. He was the last of the three to make his first-class debut doing so in 1945 – three years after his comrades-in-arms. His start did not indicate his dormant potentiality, as he made a "duck" in his first innings at No. 1 and in his first eight innings in big cricket aggregated only 133. In British Guiana, however, he showed he knew how to get three-figures at Bourda in 1946 and the following year, coming to Jamaica for the first time, he got to the 90's in the first innings of the first match at Melbourne Park and obliged with 123 in the second at Sabina Park.

Sabina Park, too, gave him his chance to reveal his potentiality as a Test batsman. Weekes was dropped after the first three Tests against England in 1948, when the illness of George Headley caused the selectors to fly the little man up from Barbados. He arrived and flew over the ground actually after the start of the fourth and final Test. A shaky start, then 141 and Weekes did not look back until he got 51 and 9 in his last Test against Pakistan at Queen's Park Oval in 1958. Undoubtedly, in his day he was the most punishing batsman in the world!

Wisden, after the 1950 tour of England, selected Weekes as one of the Five Cricketers of the year, and wrote: "Perhaps no batsman since Bradman has made such an impression on his first English tour as a ruthless compiler of big scores."

With 197 in his first Test vs. Pakistan in 1958, his characteristically slaughtering methods and wide repertoire that earned him the sobriquet of the "Butcher", remained with him up to the last – a method that at first could be encouraging to the bowler looking for a quick wicket but more often than not turned out to be so heart-breaking.

In 1950 in England he started off with 54, 3 and 0 only to follow up with 232 vs Surrey, 304 not out vs Cambridge, 279 vs Notts, 246 not out vs Hampshire, and 200 not out vs

Leicestershire. On two occasions, association with Worrell for the third wicket yielded 350 and 340 and in the Trent Bridge Test it came as "a shock" to the English that their fourth wicket tet-a-tete ended at 283 – Weekes a "mere" 129.

He averaged 56.33 for 338 runs in the Tests, and topped the season's first-class averages with 79.65 – a feat only enjoyed by one other West Indian – George Headley. His aggregate of 2,310 was only 10 short of the record of Headley in 1933, but whose 7 centuries then for a West Indian in England, Weekes equalled.

Handicapped by a pulled leg muscle, which was foolishly not allowed to mend, he averaged only 24.5 in the 1951-52 Australian Tests, but the Australians never doubted his ability and used even unnecessary bumpers when he appeared to be recovering fitness and form.

Weekes after his 141 in 1948 followed up for the still unprecedented Test sequence of 128, 194, 162 and 101 (90 run out was the next innings) against India in 1948-49. His tour first-class figures were 1,350 (av. 90) and Tests 779 (av. 111.28). In 1952-53 in the Caribbean the Indians again paid heavily with 716 (av. 102.28) and his highest Test innings ever of 207. England then did well to keep him at 8-1-487-206-69.5 in 1954 and the Australians at 10-2-469-139-58.62 in the Tests.

In New Zealand

In NZ in 1956 he set a local record with an aggregate of 940 averaging 104.44 in a season with the aid of a century each time he batted in the first 5 innings. When he was about to equal the world's record of Sir Donald Bradman and the late C.B. Fry of 6 consecutive centuries he made 43 and 56 in the sixth match. His record in the 4 Tests was 418 runs averaging 83.6 and three centuries. Appropriately with more opportunities the three Ws are the only West Indian batsmen to have compiled 10,000 runs each in firstclass cricket and Weekes' 35 centuries is a figure only passed by the other Ws.

Weekes despite his only poor tour in England 1957 is easily ahead in average in West Indian postwar cricket.

Weekes has played for Bacup (Lancashire League) each season, apart from 1950 and 1955, and has been an extremely prolific scorer, 1,518 runs (av. 89.29) in 1951 and 1,266 runs (av. 158.25) in 1954 being his best seasons. He was about the best slip fieldsman in 1950 and was always good there or at coverpoint.

WEST INDIAN SPORTSMAN - *February, 1960*

THE SHORTEST 'W' WAS
'GREATEST' WEST INDIAN

By Scyld Berry
Sunday Telegraph correspondent

WHEN SIR DONALD BRADMAN WAS ASKED by Richie Benaud what he would have averaged against England's bowling in the Ashes series last year, the Don replied "55 or 60". Richie protested, pointing out that over the span of his Test career Sir Donald had averaged 99. "Ah," he replied, "but you must remember that I'm 85."

Seeing Everton Weekes at Bourda in the last week, commentating on the second Test for Caribbean radio, was to be reminded of this anecdote. Although he is now 69, the shortest of the three W's is still so formidable in the torso that the mind's eye can still see him readily averaging 55 or 60 against England's bowling.

And perhaps—those of us who saw neither can only conjecture Weekes came closer than anyone to being a second Bradman. Certain it is, in the Don's opinion, that Weekes has been the greatest of West Indian batsmen. He was particularly withering in the crossbat strokes of pull and square-cut. Yet amid the torrent of boundaries he seldom hit the ball in the air to give the bowler a moment's hope that a fielder might catch it. Using a 2 lbs. 3oz. bat, like Frank Worrell (Clyde Walcott's was slightly heavier), he hit one six in his Test career, off a no-ball by Australia's Bill Johnston.

By his own account, he should not have toured England in 1957. He had to have a puncture made in his nose after each of the five Test matches to alleviate sinus trouble; and, during them, the mucus was causing double vision. Take away that series, and he would have averaged 64 in Test cricket, not 58.

Apart from being the shortest and most cross-batted of the three W's, Weekes came from the most disadvantaged background, in Bridgetown. "I was born and lived 500 yards from Kensington Oval. I started playing cricket at school and bowling off-breaks in the nets at Pickwick [the club which has Kensington for its home ground]."

"There was no coaching, of course," he said. "It was all done watching other players, like Derek Sealy and Lawson Bartlett." His first chances to bat in formal cricket came as L/Cpl Weekes after he bad joined the army.

The mind's eye may picture the three W's mincing attacks for many a year, both for West Indies and for Barbados. In fact, their last game together for Barbados was in 1947, in Jamaica, where Worrell stayed on to try and make a living, before moving to England to play league cricket. Weekes followed suit, playing for Bacup in the Lancashire League for seven seasons.

"I was approached to play for Kent back in the 1950s but I wasn't interested in county cricket. I believe Denis Compton was getting £700 a year, and I was getting more for playing one day a week."

On the 1950 tour of England, which established the reputations of the three W's, and Ramadhin and Valentine, Weekes savaged Cambridge University for 304 on a Fenner's pitch which he remembers as being similar to Bourda. In the Trent Bridge Test he savaged England for 261.

Maybe he would have gone on if he had possessed the burning inferiority complex of a boy from the Australian bush.

Weekes has always been ready to laugh. He's an easy companion so they say. Aged 40, after years of "relaxed living", as he calls it, he captained Barbados Colts against the 1964-65 Australians, led by Bobby Simpson. Naturally, he scored a hundred.

As part of his "relaxed living", Weekes turned Bridgetown into bridge town. He represented Barbados in the bridge Olympics and no doubt laughed and was entirely unjudgmental. But if you ask him nicely, he will pass a few judgments on England's latest defeat: "English cricket must be in bad shape if this is the best they have at the moment...

"Their bowling is ordinary without Devon Malcolm. Ian Salisbury should be encouraged, and Mark Ramprakash, but I don't think Graeme Hick is a Test player at this level. You've got Atherton, Stewart and Smith, and the captain's a bit like Len Hutton in that he can concentrate for long periods and hit the ball pretty effortlessly."

SIR EVERTON WEEKES –
MONUMENTAL INFLUENCE

*A tribute paid by Charles Alleyne to Sir Everton Weekes at the
Annual Awards Ceremony at the Sherbourne Centre on May 10,
1999. Alleyne was at one time Everton's captain at the Empire Club.*

EVERTON DECOURCEY WEEKES, K.C.M.G., G.C.M.,
O.B.E. Dooon't it sound heavy? That name is familiar all over
the world and in a dignified way even before he received his
many honours. As is his wont, he began in a humble way, first
with the O.B.E. (Officer of the British Empire), then with the
G.C.M. (Gold Crown of Merit) and later the K.C.M.G. (Knight
Commander of St. Michael and George). One feels there are
more to come.

I am honoured to be invited to say a few words on Everton's
behalf. As you should know Everton is a most organised,
determined, disciplined, confident, fearless and caring individual.
As I watched cricket in recent years and particularly during
the last Cable and Wireless Series (West Indies versus Australia)
and saw the discomfort which the Australian Glenn McGrath
caused the West Indian batsmen, I could only remember and
reflect on the discomfort which Everton caused to people like

Ray Lindwall and Keith Miller, who in my opinion, were superior to McGrath.

Everton and I have been very closely associated with each other for more than fifty years. His mother Lenora, was like a mother to me and my mother Clem, was like a mother to him. I am Godfather to his son Andy, and he is Godfather to my son, Stephen. I first met Everton when he came to the 1945 Trials at Kensington and one had to realise his class immediately. Of course he started with an advantage since the location was practically on his own doorstep. Frank and Clyde were more or less established by that time but that did not deter Everton. Indeed I believe it inspired him more. Hence his determination and confidence were immediately evident. I guess the teaching of Mr. Joe Clarke, the Headmaster of St Leonard's Boys School and the Officers the Regiment were responsible for his discipline. The attribute is known worldwide when one remembers that Everton seldom lifted the cricket ball or the football off the ground. As you know his only six boundary was at the Queen's Park Oval in Trinidad in 1955, when Everton, off a no ball from the Australian Bill Johnston, and off the back foot lifted the ball over mid–on. That was during his second innings score of 87 not out after he had scored 139 in the West Indies first innings. Everton was fearless; surely his hooking and cutting must have been as good as, if not better than, the best in the world. I believe Sir Donald Bradman, in an audience with Everton a few years ago, seemed to think so.

When one thinks today of how players can continue to be selected in West Indies teams with mediocre and poor performances and how, were it not for a stroke of luck and circumstances, the world might have been prevented from seeing the real brilliance of this star. I refer to his selection in the final Test match at Sabina Park in Jamaica in the 1947-48 Test Series, West Indies versus England, when Everton replaced George Headley, who had to withdraw from the Team. In those days, travel arrangements were not as swift and easy as they are today so you can imagine the tension and anxiety of getting Everton to Jamaica on time. As it turned out the game started before his arrival with the West Indies in the field. Surely all that must have been upsetting. However, "Little-Man" as John Goddard, who incidentally was Captain of that Test Team, used to call him, grasped the opportunity with both hands and feet, remember the twinkling toes, and scored a magnificent 141. That was the first of five consecutive centuries, the other four being scored on the 1948-49 tour of India; 128 at Delhi in November in the first Test, 194 at Bombay in the second Test in December, 162 and 101 at Calcutta in January in the third Test which established the Test Record, which seems likely to remain for evermore unbeaten. For your information, Everton scored 90 run-out at Madras in January in the fourth Test and 56 and 48 at Bombay in February in the fifth Test. I must mention that Everton seemed rather unlucky with regard to the run-out decision against him at Madras.

Tonight we are happy and proud to celebrate with Sir Everton, the Fiftieth Anniversary of his Great Achievement and Record of Five Consecutive Centuries. Generally whenever one talks of Everton Weekes one remembers that great feat. We still recall his slaughterings during the 1950 West Indies Tour of England. We remember his consistent high scores against the Indians during their tour of the West Indies during 1953-54; we will no doubt remember his consecutive scores of 123 at Dunedin, 103 at Christ Church, and 156 at Wellington during the West Indies tour of New Zealand during 1955-56. Many persons and perhaps Sir Everton himself have very high regard for the 90 he made at Lords during the West Indies. 1957 Tour of England in the second Test at Lords, when, in spite of a broken thumb and on a badly impaired pitch he withstood the likes of Statham, Trueman, Baily and Wardle. We no doubt remember his farewell to Test Cricket at Kensington when he scored a copybook 197 during the 1957- 58 Pakistan tour to the West Indies. All those were remarkable but for me I find difficulty in choosing between his 120 for Barbados against Australia at Kensington in 1955 and his 125 retired when, in 1965 at the age of 40, he was invited to Captain the Barbados Colts also against Australia.

I have never ever heard Everton make an excuse for any failure and he certainly would not wish any one to do so. However I should stress that there is perhaps no other cricketer who had to endure such handicaps as Everton did during the 1957 West Indies tour to the U.K., which was one of the few on which Everton did not make at least one century. Yet it was during that tour in spite of having several punctures to clear and ease his sinuses, that he played that brilliant innings of 90 at Lords, to which I alluded earlier. Such was the man!

Everton's many successes and his commitments and engagements, especially when he was contracted to play for Bacup in the Lancashire League, did not prevent him from looking after, or making provision for his mother to be looked after. He was deeply moved when she passed on in 1974. But like the man he is, he has "soldiered" on.

Everton has been most unselfish and he was not carried away by his successes in Jamaica in 1948, in India in 1949, in England in 1950 and I could go on and on. He has always been conscious of what he has been able to achieve through his association with the Empire Club, and I recall that shortly after his return from his vintage tour of England in 1950, he expressed a desire to tour with the Empire Club. At that time, there was no difficulty in getting acceptance from any country, once Everton Weekes was included in the touring party. Empire chose to tour Grenada in January 1951 and in the first "Test" at the Queen's Park Grounds in St. Georges, Everton scored a scintillating 150 odd. That evening he was invited to talk to a group of cricketers and modestly warned them to do as he was then advising them, but not as he had done that day. Everton is a great coach with the ability to foresee potential talent. That facility made him become quite unpopular at Empire Club in the 1959 Cricket Season, when as Captain of the First Eleven Cricket Team he dropped the late Hughley Barker, who at that stage was heading the national bowling averages, for Charlie Griffith - an unknown. I think you will agree that his choice was correct. As a coach Everton was precise and his recommendations were well thought out, uncomplicated and manageable.

Everton was an excellent leader and you will no doubt remember that he led the Barbados National Team to victory over England in the colony Match at Kensington Oval in 1960. The game is probably better remembered for the embarrassingly fast scoring rate of Cammine Smith and Conrad (now Sir Conrad) Hunte off the bowling of Statham and Trueman. But you may also recall that skipper Everton had already practically bowled his team to victory by capturing four vital wickets with leg breaks.

Everton has always been blessed with a skill of wit, tinged with a modicum of sarcasm. He has always been on the front foot to tell it like it is. He was perhaps one of, if not the best cutter in the game, so if his remarks are sometimes considered cutting why wonder? Didn't you enjoy it when he viciously cut the cricket ball past gully or point? I am sure you will join with me in wishing Sir Everton many, many more years of good health and progress.

I close with a very touching quotation of Professor Keith Sandiford of the University of Manitoba, Canada, in his famous Cricketers Series - No.29 published by the Association of Cricket Statisticians and Historians - "It was Weekes who really gave hope to the thousands of poor black youngsters in Barbados who dreamed of making something of their lives through opportunities provided by cricketing excellence. It was he who, in a sense, begat Charlie Griffith, Conrad Hunte, Seymour Nurse and Garfield Sobers. To them, he remained more than an icon, he became at once mentor, friend, father figure and role model. His place in the history of Barbadian cricket is thus secured. It rests as much on his abundant batting skills as on his monumental influence."

SIR DONALD BRADMAN, AC.

2 HOLDEN STREET.
KENSINGTON PARK,
SOUTH AUSTRALIA 5068.
12—6—91.

Dear Bob,

Thanks for your letter. Bruce Collins was here recently and filled me in with the latest news re the Museum. Like you he is full of confidence about Stage 2 going ahead but when I ask has he got the money in hand the answer is no-but I'll get it. That sounds fine but I would hate to think the project was built on borrowed money and then foundered. That would be disastrous. Anyway I'll no doubt hear more in due course.

Now re Everton Weekes. I hardly know him at all as a person but thought he was the best batsman ever to come out of the W.I. It would be a pleasure for me to meet him again. However I can hardly make a date so far ahead as next March. Looking ahead 7 days is hard for me, let alone 7 months,

I took the liberty of ringing Barry Gibbs and am assured that if Weekes and you come to Adelaide, be it for a Shield or some other match, you will both be hon. members for the day and be invited to lunch.

If you eventually decide to come on a non cricket day I would do my best to fit in with what you wish.

I think Bob we should let the matter rest there for the moment. When we are nearer the date you can contact me and we'll arrange something. I'll do my best to co—operate. I would happy about a photo. though you would somehow have to arrange for someone to take it. I'm no photographer.

I gather you all had a wonderful time in the W.I. Pity, we couldn't quite pull off a win. But it seems clear the days of W.I. invincibility are over.

Trust you are well and now back in harness.

Kindest regards,

Sincerely,

EVERTON WEEKES:
BEST OF THE W'S
By Peter West

EVERTON WEEKES and Clyde Walcott and I were at Lord's when Gordon Greenidge blazed the victory trail for West Indies with what, in the final straight, was the most spectacular batting bonanza in the history of Test cricket.

It must have been a stimulating reminder of the way they themselves plundered English bowling in 1950.

On that tour "the 3Ws" Weekes, Worrell and Walcott – took England by storm with 20 centuries between them in all the first class matches. Weekes and Walcott each made seven.

The late Sir Frank Worrell got six, including one gloriously velvet innings of 261 against England at Trent Bridge, and another double hundred, 241, not out at Leicester. But Everton de Courcy Weekes on five occasions got 200 or more.

Surridge special

During May, at the Oval, he took 232 off the Surrey bowling, including that of Alec Bedser and Jim Laker. In one passage of arms against the bowling of Surridge who had just previously signed up Weekes to sponsor Surridge bats, the first four deliveries with the second new ball were clattered for four .

"Steady on, Everton," said Jack Parker standing at slip. "You'll lose the contract." Everton played the last two balls of the over sedately down the wicket.

In the next match, at Fenners, after Cambridge University had declared at 594 for five — John Dewes (223) and David Sheppard (227) sharing an opening partnership of 345, Weekes contributed 304 not out (in 325 minutes) and Worrell 160 to a West Indies innings of 730 for three. End of match.

Everton was nearing 300 and John Warr sent down what the bowler describes as the one he reserved only for the greatest batsmen. "Look at all those people moving in front of the side screen," Everton said to Frank. "Come three."

Come, June, and Everton Weekes plundered 279 off the Nottinghamshire attack, on a bland pitch, in five minutes less than four hours.

In this murderous innings, during the course of which he never took his sweater off or broke into a sweat, he hit 43 fours. No sixes: Everton reckoned it was needlessly risky to put the ball in the air.

On his way back through the Trent Bridge pavilion, an ancient member inquired of the hero why he had not bothered to beat C.G.M McCartney's record of 345 in a day - on the same ground, for the Australians in 1921. Everton is alleged to have replied: "Man, nobody told me."

After this, he made 246 not out against Hampshire and 200 not out against Leicestershire, that last innings including the fastest hundred of the season, in 65 minutes and a partnership of 309 with Worrell in less that two and a half hours.

The West Indians made 651 for three on the first day. England's cricketers had taken first sight of Weekes when he made 118 not out for Barbados against Gubby Allen's MCC side in 1947-8. In a second game against the island, Jim Laker bowled him out cheaply with a ball that turned- a rare event on the Bridgetown pitch.

In those days, young Everton was naive. "I'd be disappointed," Laker confided to him afterwards, "if I couldn't do that once an over." In the Third Test Everton played for the turn and Laker bowled him with a ball that never got off the straight and narrow.

Deadly spin

Everton was dropped after that encounter—for the only time in his distinguished career. But he was recalled for the fourth and last Test, at Sabina Park, when George Headley was injured. In spite of some apprehension about Laker's deadly spin he achieved his first Test hundred.

Having thus got the feel of things he proceeded against India to hit four more hundreds in succession, so it was said—in his next Test innings.

"A killer", reflects J. C. Laker. "The best of the three Ws." I agree with that verdict. Worrell was the most elegant, Walcott the hardest hitter— notably off the back foot— Weekes, with his range of strokes and appetite for runs, the most devastating.

In more ways than one — in physique especially — Gordon

Greenidge evoked memories of Weekes in that Cornhill Test at Lord's. But Greenidge is not averse to hitting the ball in the air, and his shots in the cover point area are made mostly off the back foot. Everton's cover drive was a joy to behold.

Jim Laker asked him one day why he had been christened Everton. "My dad", the reply came, " was a soccer nut, and a mad keen supporter of Everton".

"A good job then," observed Jim, "that he wasn't sold on West Bromwich Albion."

CRICKET TALK
AFTER 32 YEARS OF CALYPSO
CRICKET...
THE VERY BEST OF THE WEST
– Richie Benaud

SYDNEY: West Indies Cricket has come a long a way since John Goddard in 1951–2 brought to Australia a touring team to play for the cricket championship of the world.

The West Indies had just slaughtered England in a four-match series in England and this tour was sandwiched into an Australian domestic season where originally only Sheffield Shield was to be played.

It was also the year I made my Test debut in the final game of the series, the selectors having left out Arthur Morris, Jack Moroney and Ian Johnson to try out Colin McDonald, George Thoms and your correspondent.

It was also the era of grassy pitches at the SCG and in that match, 40 wickets fell for only 784 runs. . . plenty of action, but little of it with the bat.

Lindwall, Miller and Bill Johnston took only 80 overs to

wrap up 18 of those West Indian batsmen and the game was won by a huge 202 runs.

Apart from that match, I played two Test series against the West Indies – the one in 1955 in the Caribbean and then the tied Test series in 1960-1.

But I have seen every one of the tours to England from 1963 onwards, plus their Test ventures in this country.

Their cricket has undergone a marked change in the past 30 years and in my opinion, it has very definitely been a change for the better.

They are far more professional these days than when they were playing the game as laughing cavaliers, but for most of the time, they still provide all that is best in entertainment in the game of cricket.

Cricket is the great cohesive feature of the West Indies where attempts at combining the Caribbean into one great federation of political States have been singularly unsuccessful.

Ability

Remarkably, Barbados with a population of only 13,000 in the capital Bridgetown, has produced some of the greatest cricketers the world has seen, players who have excited spectators and now television viewers in most countries of the world.

In trying to find only the best 11 players, there are certain to be some great names condemned to exclusion.

Is it really possible "those two little pals of mine – Ramadhin and Valentine" are not included?

And what of Seymour Nurse, Conrad Hunte, Alvin Kallicharran, Lawrence Rowe, and Jeff Stollmeyer? Gerry

Alexander, is the best wicket-keeper I have seen from the West Indies, but could he possibly replace in a best XI either Clive Lloyd or one of the Ws who put Barbados on the map as a cricketing nation?

At any rate, these are the 11 players I would name as the greatest I have seen from the West Indies in the past years of watching and by coincidence, they make up a team of sorts even with a possible order – I merely offer thanks that I never had to bowl against a line-up of that kind.

1. Vivian Richards,
2. Frank Worrell,
3. Rohan Kanhai,
4. Clyde Walcott,
5. Everton Weekes,
6. Clive Lloyd,
7. Garry Sobers,
8. Andy Roberts,
9. Wes Hall,
10. Michael Holding,
11. Lance Gibbs.

Both Richards and Sir Frank Worrell opened the batting successfully in their time and Kanhai was a must at No. 3, a really great batsman who delighted in a battle and loved thrashing bowlers.

Walcott, big, burly and dynamic was a contrast to the cultured Worrell and the butcher-like batting of Everton Weekes who was my pick of the three Ws. . . Walcott made a colossal 827 runs in a five-Test series against us in 1955 including five centuries.

What a player!

Clive Lloyd and Sir Garfield Sobers, would complete the batting line-up at six and seven with Sobers in the side as the all-rounder.

It is no wonder the West Indians these days are such proud cricketers when you look at that list and another 11 great players who would challenge them for a top rating – present day West Indian players have quite a bit to live up to and they do it well and in a very professional manner.